A

Countryman's

FAREWELL

A
Countryman's
FAREWELL

Or, Ninety and Counting

ROY BARRETTE

Down East Books

Text illustrations by Edith Allard

Jacket illustration: "Home," linocut by Carroll Thayer Berry (1938). Courtesy of William Conrad.

ISBN 0-89272-264-9

Library of Congress Catalog Card Number 88-51675

Designed by Edith Allard

Printed at The Book Press, Brattleboro, Vt.

5 4 3 2 1

Down East Books, Camden, Me. 04843

. . . I hold him happiest
Who before going quickly whence he came,
Hath looked ungrieving on these majesties,
The world-wide sun, the stars, water and clouds
And fire. Hast thou a hundred years to live or but
The briefest space, these thou canst always see.
Thou wilt not ever see a greater thing.
— Meander, circa 400 B.C.

I dedicate this book to all who, no matter where fate has placed them, are country folk at heart; and pray, as did Quintus Horatius Flaccus in 30 B.C., Hoc erat in votis, for "a piece of land not so very large, which would contain a garden, and near the house a spring of ever-flowing water, and beyond these a bit of wood."

Contents

Acknowledgments

No book is solely the production of its author, and it is with gratitude that I acknowledge the help, directly and obliquely, of a few of the people who have contributed to the appearance of A *Countryman's Farewell*. First is Isabel Rector Russell, who is responsible for the type-script — and additionally for keeping me from repeating myself, which old men are prone to do. Also: Lorraine Hanson, who helped meet so many deadlines in the original columns; my friends Russell Wiggins, but for whom there would be no columns, and "Pete" Miller, who buoys me up in the Berkshires; and last, but first in my affection, my wife, who never fails to question, "Have you got your column done yet?"

Introduction

I HAVE LIVED in the village of Brooklin, Maine, for thirty years—a third of my life. Children of the children who came to my door trick-or-treating in the days when I first plowed the soil in my garden or the snow from around my mailbox come now, in their turn, to solicit favors. Life in the country has more continuity than in the city; it moves more slowly, and one can without difficulty reach back into the past. Many of my neighbors live on the same land their forebears dwelt on a century ago. We are not self-sufficient (no one can be in today's interdependent world), but as a writer for a Maine magazine said of us recently, "[Brooklin] is a rare town in that most of the year-rounders who live here, work here." We have a community of interest.

I have written two previous books—and more articles and newspaper columns than I can count—in praise of my village and the tranquility I have found here. I suppose, if I were a philosopher, I could retreat into my mind and find tranquility no matter where I lived, but I am not a real philosopher, nor are most of us. The cloistered monks and nuns of old sought seclusion to meditate and talk with God. We in our village are not cloistered, and I doubt many of us talk with God, but we do not spend all our time "getting and spending," nor are we engulfed by "the madding crowd," as is the lot of those living in cities.

I suppose all authors hear from their readers; I certainly do, and particularly because of my newspaper columns. I think it significant that I do, because I do not deal with "important" matters, political, religious, or financial. What I write about, most of the time, are the small day-to-day happenings that occur in any village, and the thoughts they arouse in my mind. It is encouraging to know that so many people in this crowded world—with all its diversions, and its news of wars and rebellions—are interested in the small things that fill the days of those of us so fortunate as to live apart. I would judge that another reason I hear from my readers is because my writing is intimate, as the essay has to be to accomplish its purpose. My writing is, in a sense, autobiographical, as it reflects the writer's views. I am glad if seeing something through my eyes opens a window that might otherwise have remained closed. My excuse for writing as I do is contained in Henry

David Thoreau's remark in *Walden* that "I should not talk so much about myself if there were anybody else whom I knew as well."

I grow old, so this will, I am reasonably sure, be the last of the *Countryman* books, making a trilogy. In the New Testament, the disciple John said, "The night cometh when no man can work." My old English teacher Cornelius Weygandt called *his* last book *The Edge of Evening*, and as I am much older than he was, I am long past the edge of evening. All I can see is the afterglow in the western sky. I remember, though, that Thomas Fuller wrote that "it is always darkest just before the dawn," so if there is a fourth book, I can call it *A Countryman's Resurrection*.

SPRING

Come, gentle Spring, aethereal Mildness, come,
And from the bosom of yon dropping cloud,
While music wakes around, veil'd in a shower
Of shadowing roses, on our plains descend.
 —from The Seasons, by Mr. Thomson,
London 1730

Spring

Wᴿɪᴛᴇʀs, Pᴏᴇᴛs Esᴘᴇᴄɪᴀʟʟʏ, are fond of talking about the miracle of spring. I am sure I have done so myself. It sounds well and gives us something we can use to try to describe a wonderful and beautiful occurrence, but when you get right down to it, nothing that happens with such predictability, and has so happened for millions of years, can properly be termed a miracle. Miracles don't appear on schedule. Nevertheless, I am stirred by it every year, and as many times as I have experienced it, the season still takes me by surprise.

I am sure that cavemen, living in the temperate zones, responded with relief to the arrival of spring. We know that Stonehenge and the temples in Mexico, thousand of miles apart, were built with some accuracy to measure the passage of the seasons, but what awes me, when I ponder on it, is that spring spread across the earth each year aeons before man arrived to witness it.

However, the evidence of spring that I enjoy is on a somewhat lesser scale, even though I know the celestial occurrences that bring it about. Long before even the most adventurous snowdrop pierces the frozen ground, there are earlier signs heralding spring's approach. On the domestic level we drink our afternoon tea by daylight, and no longer feel called upon to

> Sᴛɪʀ ᴛʜᴇ ꜰɪʀᴇ, ᴀɴᴅ ᴄʟᴏsᴇ ᴛʜᴇ sʜᴜᴛᴛᴇʀs ꜰᴀsᴛ,
>
> Lᴇᴛ ꜰᴀʟʟ ᴛʜᴇ ᴄᴜʀᴛᴀɪɴs, ᴡʜᴇᴇʟ ᴛʜᴇ sᴏꜰᴀ ʀᴏᴜɴᴅ,
>
> Aɴᴅ ᴡʜɪʟᴇ ᴛʜᴇ ʙᴜʙʙʟɪɴɢ ᴀɴᴅ ʟᴏᴜᴅ-ʜɪssɪɴɢ ᴜʀɴ
>
> Tʜʀᴏᴡs ᴜᴘ ᴀ sᴛᴇᴀᴍʏ ᴄᴏʟᴜᴍɴ, ᴀɴᴅ ᴛʜᴇ ᴄᴜᴘs
>
> Tʜᴀᴛ ᴄʜᴇᴇʀ ʙᴜᴛ ɴᴏᴛ ɪɴᴇʙʀɪᴀᴛᴇ ᴡᴀɪᴛ ᴏɴ ᴇᴀᴄʜ,
>
> Sᴏ ʟᴇᴛ ᴜs ᴡᴇʟᴄᴏᴍᴇ ᴘᴇᴀᴄᴇꜰᴜʟ ᴇᴠᴇɴɪɴɢ ɪɴ,

as William Cowper instructed us. Also, I awaken earlier every morning because my bedroom is flooded with light by five o'clock.

Outdoors I see the Canada geese heading north in a wavering arrow, even though ice still rims the ponds; and just a couple of nights ago while I was driving home from Blue Hill, a skunk ambled across the road in front of me in that unconcerned manner skunks assume. When I looked across the hayfield this morning, forty to fifty birds were feeding among the stubble. I thought at first they were grackles, because I had seen a dozen or so perched like black fruit in an old wild apple tree, but after watching them a few minutes I decided they were robins. I was too far away to distinguish their rusty breasts, but there is no mistaking the way a robin walks: it takes a sort of half-hop and three or four quick steps, then stops with its head cocked to one side while it looks and listens. I didn't see any robins bracing themselves back to extract an elastic worm, so I suppose they were feeding on something else. (The top few inches of ground are thawed but beneath that it is frozen, and I doubt that there are any worms.) I am always encouraged by the sight of some early robins. I know they are not trustworthy weather prophets, for occasionally they get caught in a late snowstorm, but on the whole, when robins appear, can spring be far behind?

I found another sign yesterday when my wife and I were squelching along over the half-frozen ground in the kitchen garden. No, it was not rhubarb or asparagus we saw, but a new, small pussy willow sent to me as a gift from the Arnold Arboretum in Boston a few years ago. It is still only a couple of feet tall, but nevertheless large enough to display some catkins. Its name is *Salix melanostachys*, but we have rechristened it "the black pussy willow" as being easier to say and remember. The "pussies" are small, no longer than half an inch, and if you hold one in your hand it looks and feels like some small insect.

If you live in a city, the only way you know spring is approaching is by the bunches of daffodils for sale in the supermarkets. The sidewalks aren't squashy, and you can't smell the unmistakable fragrance of soil growing warmer under the influence of a sun that climbs higher every day. I guess it *is* a miracle, after all; it is for those of us lucky enough to live in the country, anyway. If spring came but once in a hundred years, likewise the robins, the whole world would stand in awe and wonder.

I am writing this on the fifteenth of March, the Ides of March that Caesar told us to beware of, though I see nothing foreboding this year. It is, as a matter of fact, the first day of sunshine in two weeks that has moved me to circumnavigate my garden. I took my secateurs with me—I carry them wherever I go in the garden, as a police officer carries his sidearm—and was able to use them to gather a small bouquet. Some might quarrel with the term bouquet, as it did not contain the kind of flowers that might be bought in a flower shop. This bouquet, however, was a harbinger of spring, and now brightens up the parlor, where it is displayed on a coffee table.

You will want to know what is in my bouquet (or I shall want you to, which is to the same purpose) so without too much reluctance I shall tell you. There are several twigs of Chinese witch hazel, *Hamamelis mollis*, which has been blooming on warm days for the last month; some small pieces of the black pussy willow, *Salix melanostachys*; and a couple of stiff twigs of the white variety of the February Daphne. This, botanically, is *Daphne Mezereum*, and I love it because it will open overnight to waft a delicious fragrance abroad. (Note: You can buy the willow from Wayside Gardens, and they list also *Hamamelis X intermedia*, Arnold Promise, which is a cross between *H. mollis* and *H. japonica* and should be as good, or perhaps better, than *H. mollis*. I have searched my catalogues and cannot help you with *Daphne Mezereum*; lots of other daphnes are listed that are as fragrant but do not bloom as early as the February Daphne.)

Closer to earth I found a few snowdrops and a couple of the early species crocuses. They are yellow and tissue-paper fragile but, if snowed on, will close their petals and wait for the snow to melt. I am sorry I cannot tell you their name, because they have been brightening my springs for twenty years. Their label, if ever they had one, is long gone, but I suspect they are *Crocus ancyrensis*. Each little corm you plant has up to a couple of dozen small yellow flowers. The bulbous iris, *I. reticulata*, and some of the early daffodils, the tiny ones, are through the ground and await only a few more days of sunshine to spread their petals.

You might wonder why I am wandering around, blowing on my frozen fingers, in search of modest flowers when I have in my greenhouse a number of quite spectacular amaryllis; a great many freesias that have been particularly lovely and fragrant this year (except the blue ones, which are pretty but scentless), and any number of odds and ends of geraniums and impatiens and suchlike, which will go outdoors when the nights are warm enough, although that won't be for some months yet. The reason is that while a greenhouse may be filled with flowers and burgeoning with seedlings that await the day they can be transplanted, it is nevertheless a besieged citadel, with winter on one side of a fragile piece of glass and an ever-threatened summer on the other. What is growing inside tells me nothing of the progress of the seasons. The hibiscus with its enormous tropical flowers, the bougain-villea reminding me of a house I used to visit in Mexico, tell me noth-ing of spring. To find *that* I have to put on my boots and stumble through the wasting snowdrifts to where I can smell the damp earth and see the swelling buds of the beeches silhouetted against my pale northern sky. I have to see the pussy willows swelling where they grow in the roadside ditches, and wonder at how green the grass is where snow has lain drifted all winter.

I know, too, where very soon I shall find the hard purple spathes of skunk cabbages forcing their way through the frozen mud of the swamp that lies in one place along my shoreline. Experiments have been made showing a higher temperature within the spathe than in the surrounding ground. In 1878 L. Prang and Company of Boston published several volumes of a work by a Pennsylvanian named Thomas Meehan, entitled Native Flowers and Plants, which contains a long description of the skunk cabbage. If your library has this book you might be interested in reading it. The entry is too long to quote in full, but in one place Meehan says: "for plants are in some respects like animals, and must keep up a certain degree of heat, no matter how low the temperature may be about them." Plants seem to have anti-freeze in their veins. Onions, for instance, will survive temperatures that would freeze us as stiff as marble.

So here I am indoors again by my coal fire, keeping warm by the burning of vegetation that grew on earth a hundred million years ago, and patiently awaiting yet another spring.

Cindy

Almost Anything Can, and does, appear in my essays: butchering sheep, growing chrysanthemums, what I think of old age, book reviews, travelogues ("Adventures in Contentment," as David

Grayson would have called them), and just about everything that flits across my mind or happens to me. What started as a piece devoted to gardening turned into a record of what goes on in a man's head. That happened long ago—in 1966, to be exact—and circumstances haven't changed since. Apparently this makes no difference to my readers. What interests me in my mail is that while a good many of the letters come from people in middle or later life, these are by no means predominant. Recently I heard from a girl of fifteen who wanted to work for me this summer; from another young woman admitting to thirty-three who said how much she had learned from another elderly gardener and how she enjoyed sharing my thoughts; another cheerful person of eighty-five and still going strong, who urged me to keep writing; and still another reminding me that her husband doctored my cows twenty years ago.

The last episode I remember very well. We had, at that time, a cow named Cindy. She was a Guernsey, very placid and an easy milker. Time passed, and Cindy freshened right on time. She had her calf, but it was obvious that she was not very well. I didn't recognize what was wrong, but Aunt Bessie, who lived down the road a piece and was knowledgeable about cattle, did: Cindy had milk fever, and what I had to do, fast, was to get a veterinarian. All of this happened late at night, so I called my friend Harlow Cameron who lived sixty miles away, and, with a state trooper riding shotgun, he got here in under an hour. In the meanwhile Aunt Bessie said we should not let Cindy lie down, which was what she most of all wanted to do. We tried to prop her up with bales of hay and succeeded to a degree, but by the time Harlow got there she had slid down, with her head on my wife's lap. Helen couldn't move because eleven hundred pounds of Guernsey had her pinned down. Although in those days I could still sling forty-pound bales of hay around like basketballs, I couldn't do much with half a ton of cow.

The cure for milk fever is dramatic. The veterinarian pulled out of his bag a syringe about as big as a fire extinguisher, filled it with calcium, and punched it into Cindy's jugular. For a couple of minutes nothing happened, then the cow moved her head—enabling Helen to escape, which she did with alacrity. We were all in the calving pen together and removed ourselves promptly. Suddenly Cindy struggled to her feet, with hooves and bales of hay flying in all directions. She wavered around for a bit and then staggered over to her calf, which she proceeded to clean up. In another few minutes she looked quite normal, and when I went into the pen to give her a pail of warm water, she stared at me in a puzzled way, asking as clearly as a cow could, What in hell is all the excitement about? What is everybody doing down here in the middle of the night?

Cindy had several more calves, and every time she did, she got milk fever. I understand that nowadays calcium can be given as a preventative, but it was not the procedure then, so once a year—usually in the middle of the night—I would call Harlow and say, "Cindy's done it again," and he would rush down to the farm and give emergency treatment. Eventually I sold her, which made me sad, because even though she was only a "three-titter" and got milk fever regularly, she was a friend and I knew what was going to happen to her.

To answer my various well-wishers who seem to be concerned about my age and staying power, I want to say that as long as my publishers indulge me and I have strength to sit at my typewriter, my weekly message of good cheer will continue to burst upon a startled world (its author being as surprised as its readers that he met another deadline).

Pruning

ALTHOUGH SNOW STILL covers the big perennial border and is drifted deep in the lee of the hedges and stone walls, the ground is clear where the sun shines. I have been looking longingly out of my kitchen window at the scattering of crocuses showing tiny rags of yellow under the old lilac, where they follow close on the edge of the wasting snow bank, and have been aching to get out to prune the crab apple trees in the formal garden. Yesterday I decided to venture forth. The temperature was up to forty degrees and there was not much wind, but the ground was still soggy, something a good stiff breeze will soon remedy. Nancy, who keeps house for us, heard me say I was going out and warned me to put on my boots. I did, and as I practically live in them from November to March, I felt about as usual.

Although my crab apple trees are not large—I planted them only twenty-five years ago, and ornamental crabs do not grow very fast—I had to do a lot of the pruning with a ten-foot pole pruner, which is an awkward tool to handle. One of several disadvantages to using it is that to reach the top branches I have to stand close to the tree and look into the sky. About ten minutes of that and my neck feels as though I had been suffering what the law calls "hanging by the neck until you be dead." The job would be done a bit easier from the top of a ladder, but I did not want to dig holes in the lawn, which my weight on the ladder would certainly have accomplished, and I am not so agile on the top of a fruit-picking ladder as I once was. However, to balance the pain of a stiff neck, I had, on the ground, the comfort of knowing I couldn't fall off.

I don't know if everyone gets the same pleasure out of spring that blesses me. Perhaps it is reserved only for gardeners and country dwellers, but even though the ground is still cold and the only things in bloom are the pussy willows and witch hazels, there is a certain quality to the light and a very real taste to the air that is wine to my spirit. There is also the arrival of the birds from their southern journeyings, and the change in manner of the winter residents. It is a bit early yet, but soon the goldfinches will don their yellow vests, so that birds that have looked like dull little sparrows all winter will quite suddenly turn into golden balls swinging against the blue of the sky as though on pendulums. (They sing on the down beat, you will notice.)

Another reward I gathered from stumbling around that tree with my head in the air like a bittern, was seeing my second flock of Canada geese this year. There were about fifty of them flying in a one-sided arrow, ten on one side and forty on the other. They were too high for me to hear their trumpeting, if indeed they were conversing (they do not always do so), but they were headed down the coast where, if they could not find an open pond, they could alight on sheltered salt water, as the ice is out of most of the bays.

My trees were not pruned last year, and as a result vertical suckers have grown so strongly from the upper branches, the canopy, that they look like the quills on a porcupine. These things are small in diameter and thus easy to cut, but because there are so many, they are tiring and tedious to remove. It should be done, though, for ornamental trees in a formal garden must conform to the formality; they are a part of the picture and, besides, flowers occur on short spurs and not on long, leggy growth.

I think I first gained my affection for formally trained trees when I saw them in Paris. The French are great for formality and don't like their vegetation wandering off anywhere it chooses. Many of you have, I am sure, seen the surroundings of Versailles and perhaps the gardens of Vaux-le-Vicomte or Villandry that are so magnificent. (Villandry is a re-creation of a Renaissance garden.) The same sense of French garden discipline is created by their long country roads lined with vertical poplars reaching like exclamation points toward heaven. On a much smaller scale, but retaining all the quality of a French garden, was one I saw on the outskirts of Philadelphia. The house and garden were owned by a man who had been our ambassador to France. He too had fallen under the spell of the great château gardens and had very successfully re-created their feeling on a lesser scale. His house was a small replica of a modest château, mansard roof and all, and its paved forecourt was graced with four rigidly pruned trees like those in my garden. He was more successful than I have been, not only because his house and forecourt were in style, but because he had been more severe with his pruning knife. One cannot straddle the issue of whether to have a "naturalistic" tree or one that is formally shaped. I am afraid that mine are of the former, but, juggling the pruner around this morning, I was encouraged to lop more severely in order to save myself work later. It is easier to take off a fair-sized overgrowth of branch than to have to fiddle around with a lot of twigs.

Anyway, the real reward is in being able to get outdoors on an early spring morning, remembering Shakespeare's warning, "Now 'tis the spring, and weeds are shallow-rooted; / Suffer them now and they'll o'ergrow the garden."

Happy

SOME TV PROGRAMS contain a warning that they depict scenes that may disturb you, and if you are unwilling to expose yourself to them you should turn to another channel. While there is nothing in this essay that is objectionable, it is intended for—and can be understood only by—dog lovers. I do not mean people who keep a dog tied on a rope in the back yard, but those for whom their dog is a part of the family.

A long time ago, twelve or fourteen years perhaps, I wrote an essay around the passing of my dog Quince. It is preserved in my book *A Countryman's Journal,* and while enough time has passed that I can now read it dry-eyed, it still brings back to me a sadly sweet memory of my old companion. I have always thought it to be one of my better efforts, because it came from my heart. My friend Andy (E. B.) White told me it was the only "dog piece" he had ever been able to read that did not make him want to upchuck. I hope this one would also be thought of by him in that way, were he around to read it.

In the piece mourning Quince's death, I made mention of my wife's little Brittany spaniel puppy, Happy. Now, because dogs die too soon, or man lives too long, I am once again grief-stricken—this time for Happy, who died in the fullness of her years, a week ago. It is only now that I am composed enough to write of her. She was a Southern lady, born on a plantation in South Carolina on May 20, 1972, who came to live with us July 25 of that same year. From then until the time of her death, we were seldom parted. She was a good traveler and we took her almost everywhere with us, selecting our lodgings by the proprietor's willingness to accept Happy. One of the few times we traveled abroad and had to leave Happy behind, her concern with our absence was equalled only by her joy at our return. Although after the death of Quince we found a companion for her, another Brittany spaniel we named Gay, Happy kept her own special place in our affection and we in hers.

Happy had been ill for some time, suffering from the usual impairments of old age: cardiovascular problems, arthritis, etc., yet her death was not anticipated until a few weeks ago. She grew weaker, but no less affectionate. Toward the end, she could not jump onto the foot of my wife's bed where she had been accustomed to sleep at night. I tried helping her, but we couldn't make it—because I too have my problems—so she took to sleeping on the rug at the foot of the stairs, where she could check on our movements. I don't think she worried as we did, because man is the only animal that knows it will someday die.

It was I who decided when. I have made few more difficult decisions. I knew Happy would be terrified if we took her to a veterinarian's office; besides, it would be undignified. We asked the veterinarian to come to us, so Happy could make the great leap from life to death in her own home under familiar surroundings, with those she had known so long beside her. It was soon done. She made no slightest objection. I took her head in my hands as I have done many thousands of times, she looked trustingly in my eyes, and in a few seconds her head grew heavy. It was over. I am an old man and not unacquainted with death, but its speed and finality overcame me. Her body was warm, her eyes open and still on mine, but the spirit was gone; I felt as though I should have seen it depart. I went to my room to hide my grief.

A friend, knowing of my affection for dogs, brought me a framed appreciation of them written by the Irish dramatist and novelist St. John Ervine. I know from the letters I have received over the years that many of my readers are dog lovers too, so I will share this with you.

I hope that I retain my reason about dogs, but whether I do or not, I know this, that I would not be without these animals at any price. Their companionship is delightful, and their affection extraordinarily moving. To be welcomed home by three little dogs that wag their tails and utter barks of pleasure at one's return is among the happiest experiences a man can enjoy. It is a happiness I do not intend, if I can help it, ever to forego. There are people, and I am sorry for them, to whom a dog is only a nuisance. Well, they have their nature, and it is absurd to complain of them for it, but they are unenviable. They are missing a great happiness.

I don't have three little dogs, but I had two that were sort of middle-sized. They did indeed wag their tails and wildly welcome us home, even if the extent of our journey had only been the few miles to the village. I don't know about a dog's conception of time; I think it varies. At one extreme they are sad at your absence but sure you will be back soon, and, at the other, they give up hope of ever seeing you again when you have been gone for several weeks. We don't travel much these days but I can remember that when we had been gone for a long time, Happy would not just bark her joy at our return but would actually cry, and crawl into my lap to prevent my leaving again.

People who do not live with dogs know nothing about them, while we who do are apt to be bemused and to attribute human characteristics to our pets, and to anthropomorphize them (as we do God). The truth probably is that in some respects dogs have talents and intelligence beyond our understanding while in others—reasoning, perhaps—we are their superiors. The longer I live, though (and I have lived a long time, most of it with dogs as companions), the more am I convinced that the difficulty we sometimes have in understanding dogs is not lack of intelligence on either of our parts, but rather a difficulty in communicating, as though one spoke an obscure Himalayan dialect and the other Gaelic. The area where we come together is in affection, in love, which is, after all, where we can meet dogs, as well as people, on common ground.

Rhubarb

WELL, WE SEEM to have battled successfully up the long slope of March hill, but the muddy plateau of April lies ahead before we gain the flowery meads of May. However, spring or not, gardening calls. When I was in the bank recently a young lady for whom I have a considerable affection asked when I was going to write on the subject of spring. She said she did not think much of my literary essays, wrinkling up her nose as she told me. So, being an accommodating fellow, particularly where pretty young ladies are concerned, I'll have at it.

As everybody who lives in New England knows, early spring is a time of hope and frustration. With our horticultural batteries recharged by floods of seed catalogues, we sally bravely forth to plant our early peas (Frosty, maybe?) and, thrusting our digging forks into the ground, we strike permafrost. The only wise thing to do is to go back indoors, mix up a warm drink, heist your feet up in front of the stove that your wife was sensible enough to keep burning in spite of your spring madness (all warm-blooded animals have periods of spring idiocy), and plug in the seed catalogues for a couple more weeks.

There are those who talk about pussy willows and alder catkins, snowdrops and skunk cabbages, as being the harbingers of the burgeoning year, but for me, spring is not really here until I can don my galoshes and hie me to the garden to pull the earliest rhubarb and cut the first adventurous spikes of the tenderest asparagus. I know all about the pioneers like Euell Gibbons who open the season by whittling icy dandelions out of the frozen lawn and emulate the Indians by wading into the frigid mud of a pond to pull the tiny tubers of the arrowheads with their bare toes, but I prefer domesticated vegetables that, like my sheep and my hens, I can keep corralled behind a fence until it suits my purpose to make a meal of them.

Speaking of rhubarb, we have a lot of last year's still on hand. It freezes so easily that we always put up more than we can use. There is no blanching or other fussing with the raw product; all we do is cut it into pieces about an inch long, wash it, put in into plastic bags, and pop it into the freezer. When we cook rhubarb we usually add frozen strawberries and sugar. (The strawberries give it elegance.) If it is to be used as a dessert, a little heavy cream or sour cream at the table doesn't do any harm, but for breakfast I prefer it straight.

There is not much to choose between fresh and frozen rhubarb except for the very pink and tender first stalks that we force by placing a barrel or box over them. This is the sort of rhubarb that sells for astronomical figures in the fancy-food stores but is easy enough to produce at home. All you need do is knock the ends out of a barrel about three feet tall, set it over the root you want to force, cover the top with boards to keep out the light, put a rock on it, and the job is done. (The rock is to prevent the boards from blowing off or being shoved off by the growing rhubarb.) This won't give you an earlier crop, but will produce those elegant, tender, coral-pink stalks.

We grow two kinds of rhubarb at Amen Farm, but as I didn't buy either of them I am not sure of the varieties. The larger, which always shocks visitors because it grows about four feet tall with leaves like umbrellas, I rescued from under a pile of builder's rubbish when we were making the house habitable, many years ago. I noticed one spindling stalk topped by an anemic yellow leaf, struggling to reach the daylight, so I dug it out, planted it with a generous mulch of cow manure, and it has never looked back. I have split it several times and given away several clumps, but it still reigns triumphant, the biggest thing around.

A few years ago, when a friend was having a garden wedding, I let the rhubarb flower; the flower stalks were five or six feet tall and were used as a kind of reredos behind the alfresco altar.

Our other variety of rhubarb is much smaller and looks more like rhubarb is supposed to look. I grow it because the stalks are deep red all the way through, and, served by itself, it makes a very pretty and delicate dessert. I think it is a Canadian variety but as it came to me through the generosity of a friend who lived on Grindstone Neck, I call it "Grindstone," which confuses people from away. The difference in size between these two varieties is genetic and has nothing to do with the manure that I apply unstintingly to both.

There are about twenty species of rhubarb (*Rheum*, botanically) but the culinary variety is probably a hybrid. Rhubarb has been around for a long time, but only recently has it been eaten. In earlier days the root was used medicinally. The story goes that in 1810 an English gardener sent five bunches of rhubarb to the local market but had to take back two, because nobody knew what it was or wanted it. Rhubarb did not become popular for quite some time—which is not surprising, because in the beginning several people made the mistake of eating the leaves and were poisoned. The leaves are indeed quite lethal.

The old herbalists recommended a tincture of rhubarb as a spring tonic and it was still so used in my boyhood. Our old herbalist friend, John Gerard, after giving detailed instructions about how to make an infusion of rhubarb root (which included, incidentally, steeping it in four gallons of strong ale for three days), says of rhubarb: "Being alwais carefull to keep a good diet: it purifieth the bloud and makes yong wenches look faire." No guarantee goes with this.

Lettuce

ACCORDING TO THE Beaufort Scale, a moderate gale is from thirty-two to thirty-eight knots. This is something over thirty-six statute miles per hour, nothing to get excited about, but something you can lean against. A moderate gale is what has been blowing here for the past three days. The wind has been out of the northwest, which, if you were to follow it back far enough, would land you on the arctic ice. It is a cold wind, summer or winter. In the winter it will drive the thermometer down to twenty degrees below zero in a hurry, and even on a warm summer day it sends the ladies scurrying for their wraps. This northwest wind is what persuaded "the money" to migrate to the Maine coast for the summer, in the days before air-conditioning, and it is the reason that hordes of tourists come today. Even with air-conditioners you can't cool all outdoors, but that northwest wind—together with a sea temperature that never gets much above fifty-four degrees—takes care of the problem handily.

When I am in England I listen to my friends complain about "that vicious east wind that chills to the marrow." It does, too, as it comes off the vast flat stretches of arctic Russia. While it does not drive their thermometers down to twenty degrees below zero, there is something about their east wind that is particularly raw and bone-chilling. The fact that it is a dry wind coming over land, just as our west winds blow over land, accounts for the biting character. Winds off the water—west for Europe, east for America—modify the extremes of temperature and provide the moisture to make lawns green and flowers bloom. Here in Maine, the easterlies bring snow in winter and rain and fog in summer, but they keep coastal areas ten or fifteen degrees warmer in winter and cooler in summer than it is a few miles inland.

The reason I was worrying about a northwest gale was because I planted my lettuce out on April 9 (which, if you don't live around here, you may not recognize as a rash and foolhardy act.) Usually we get frosts into May, sometimes late May, and the month of April is closer to winter than to summer. Of course, I didn't just plant the lettuce and pray; I have learned the Lord wastes little time on fools. I set the small plants out under cloche. My cloches are descendants of the bell-glasses French gardeners used, to grow early greens for the Paris market. Originally they were shaped like a bell, hence the name "cloche," which is to say, "hat." Mine are not round, but are made of four panes of glass hooked together by wires, and they look like small barns. There are plastic cloches but I prefer the glass ones, for in a moderate gale the plastic ones get blown off into the next county.

The first night of the northwester the temperature dropped to twenty-eight degrees. I went out the next morning with some trepida-

tion but found all was well; there was a little crust of frost in the ground outside the cloches, but the soil inside was still unfrozen. It must have been a close call. As the day wore on, and the sky got clearer and the wind blew harder, I got more apprehensive, so before Ivar (our gardener) went home I asked him to cover the row of cloches with a piece of heavy green plastic that we had in the barn and to shovel some earth up on the sides to keep it anchored. When I got up early the next morning, the thermometer read twenty degrees. In a little while Ivar came in and told me he had peeked in the end of the row of cloches and everything seemed all right. We left the plastic on all the next day and night, but on the third morning, when I awoke to the sound of rain, we removed it and the plants were none the worse for their experience.

If you are a gardener and enjoy early lettuce from your garden—and how much better really fresh lettuce is than the battle-scarred stuff you get in the supermarket—raise a few plants, and take a chance and plant them out too early. With protection that your ingenuity can devise from a dozen different things, you may win. If you lose—well, that is what life is all about, isn't it?

I have, at one time or another, grown about every variety lettuce known to man and still grow three or four, and try all the ones. The variety I planted in this experiment (and found to be hardy and a wonderful lettuce in every respect) is similar to crunch, only larger and of a deeper color. It is called Manoa introduced by Northrup King Seeds of Fresno, California; th to be found in many retail hardware and seed stores.

Still and Cool

I AWAKEN EARLY these days. My bedr o'clock and it is not long before I get up and what the new day offers. About all I could red eye of Bass Harbor light ten miles aw

white on Flye Island. The sky was clear and I wondered if the frost had nipped my lettuce. The thermometer dropped to thirty-four degrees last night, and that is near enough to freezing to scare me.

After my survey I climbed back into bed and hoped for another nap, but failing that, satisfied myself with enjoying the wonderful familiarity of my surroundings. Even in the semidarkness I could distinguish the objects I have lived with for so many years and, as always, found them comforting and an antidote for the small concerns that assail us in the nighttime. Pictures and furniture and draperies may be inanimate objects, and the way the swelling dawn etches the outline of a door panel may not be thought important, but they are reassuring evidence of predictability in an increasingly unpredictable world.

When I was young I worried more than I do now. I can remember lying in bed once for several hours, troubled about whether or not I had done something I was supposed to do in my office. I finally got up and dressed and drove fifteen miles into the city at two in the morning to satisfy myself. Now, years later, I do not even recall the problem.

It is trite to say that most of the things we worry about never happen but it is nonetheless true, and I think one has to grow old to accept it. What I do nowadays, instead of fretting, is to stay quietly in my bed appreciating all my comforts and blessings. First of all is the simple fact of being able to lie warm and unafraid, in familiar surroundings, listening to the many night noises of an old house. Most of creation is not so fortunate. I have not always been so myself. But familiarity dulls the edge of remembrance, and unless we take ourselves by the hand back along the path of the past, we soon take our present blessings for granted.

As time passes we see things from a different angle and in a differnt light. Out attitudes and responses to living are established by ents long-gone—and we think forgotten—but which nevertheless 'or our responses. Because I was once bitten by a lamb into whose uth I had foolishly thrust a finger for it to suck, I never see a sheep I am reminded of the event. This is a happy memory though, for ite was but a pinch, and the reminder brings also a picture of a ooded day in the country. I had been fishing, and laid down my t a moment to wander over to a fence and the lamb. The water arkling, the grass green, and all the new leaves that soft mixture rs only present at the break of the year.

A Countryman's Farewell

18

I have that same feeling for the country that surrounds me here in Maine, particularly when, as now, the wild pear is a billowing veil of blossom and the new leaves of the trees and shrubs are so tender you wonder how they can ever mature into what will be a blazing carpet of gold and red and bronze in the fall.

I am not a religious man in the formal sense of the word, but I never think about the beauty and order that surround us without feeling that behind this world, and around it, there is an unseen universe greater and less comprehensible than anything man can conceive. It is not a world of science, nor of religious "faith," but an all-enveloping oneness we all share and will never know anything more about.

Something there is, in my country I love so well, that is comforting and embracing, something that confers a benediction, if only one will be still long enough for it to work its charm.

Just as all wild things will come if only you will sit without moving at the edge of a wood, so what Christians call "the peace that passeth all understanding" will settle around you if you will, as George Fox, the English Quaker suggested, "be still and cool in thy own mind and spirit." Easier perhaps for the old than the young, but worth pursuing at any age.

Roses

NOT EVERYONE WHO reads this will have roses in bloom, yet he must, if he loves them, recall the opening sentence of *A Book About Roses*, by S. Reynolds Hole, the Dean of Rochester and the first great modern rosarian. It says, "He who would have beautiful roses in his garden must have beautiful roses *in his heart*." It is an old-fashioned book (published in 1901), and the specific roses mentioned, except for a very few, are now but fragrant memories. However, if you follow what is said about *growing* roses you won't go far wrong, and will have them as soon as the weather permits.

I don't grow many roses except the shrub types here at Amen Farm, because neither our soil nor climate is ideal, and I have long since lost interest in growing something just to be able to say I beat the odds. I would not, however, want you to think I do not agree with Dean Hole. I have in the past grown beautiful roses in other gardens, and still do in my heart. I have a big garden here, and roses should be the *pièce de résistance* of small ones. They are intimate flowers, to be observed at close range, and their fragrance and femininity encourage one to gather and place them in a crystal vase where they are at one's elbow.

As most of my friends know, I once lived not far from Philadelphia, where the soil and climate are almost perfect for rose-growing. When I first moved there as a young married man, I rented a house in a nearby suburb. It was not much of a house but was all I could afford, a stucco, semidetached, jerry-builder's dream. The house was on a lot twenty-five feet wide, and the front "garden" was a six-foot bank where the subsoil from the cellar excavation had been bulldozed to get it off what was to be the street. The front door was reached by a flight of steep concrete steps. In back of the house was a rather larger space where they had spread the rest of the subsoil. It was about as unpromising a situation for a garden as any I have faced.

The first thing I did was to plant a pair of *Spirea prunifolia*, Bridal Wreath, on either side of the front steps, and in three years they had foamed into fountains of white. The back garden, though, was a problem. I didn't want just annuals, some of which will grow almost anywhere, but of all things, I craved roses. No one but I thought roses would grow in such an unpromising situation, but they did—and they flourished because roses actually do well in a heavy clay soil if they are properly planted and fed.

At the risk of belaboring the point, I would repeat that at that time I was not very well supplied with this world's goods. I knew I needed manure to prepare the soil for my roses, so I gathered it from the road with a pail and a little coal shovel. In those antediluvian days bread, ice, and milk, as well as a few other commodities, were delivered by horse-drawn wagons. There were not many trucks, and horses were considered superior anyway, because after they had been over a route a few times they would keep pace with the delivery man without his having to get aboard. I think all the horses that made deliveries in my neighborhood recognized me as I scouted the byways for their leavings. I would not go to the length of saying they consciously did their best for me, but it was not long before I stood in considerable debt to them.

Constricted though my budget was, I found room for a three-dollar membership in the Pennsylvania Horticultural Society, whereby in addition to the use of their fine library, I received the magazine *Horticulture* twice a month. I read it avidly and took particular notice of the advertisements, among which was one of Bobbink and Atkins, a rose-growing firm in Rutherford, New Jersey. From them I bought a half-dozen roses, which I planted in my subsoil clay enriched by the contribution of the iceman's horse. I can still remember the names of three of them: one was Madame Butterfly, another Kaiserin Augusta Victoria, and the third was Independence Day. Madame Butterfly was a lovely gold-shaded pink; Kaiserin Augusta probably the most refined and beautiful white rose ever grown; and Independence Day, a copper color that has never been duplicated. (These last two were rather weak of growth, but people then did not have roses like Peace, which has canes like walking sticks, to compare them with.)

In those days, roses—whether purchased from a nursery or a mail-order firm—were delivered bare-root. The season when they could be planted was limited and planting had to be more carefully done than it is now, when with a pre-planted rose you just dig a hole and drop it in. It was a bit more trouble then, but plants did better.

Bare-root roses can still be had from mail-order nurseries and early spring is when you should order them. If you cannot plant them immediately when they arrive, store them in a cool, frost-free place and make sure the wrapping around the roots is kept moist. When you are ready to plant, trim off any dead or broken roots and tops, and soak the roots in a pail of water enriched by about one-quarter-strength soluble fertilizer for twenty-four hours. Dig a *big* hole, mound the earth in the bottom into a cone, and drape the roots over it. Half fill the hole with the topsoil you saved when you dug it, firm in with your feet, and fill with water. When the water has drained away, fill the hole with soil to ground level. From then on, keep it moderately moist until growth starts.

If you follow this procedure with bare-root roses, you will wind up with better and longer-lived plants than if you used pre-potted ones. Pre-potting is for the nurseryman's benefit because it lengthens the season of sale and attracts the impulse buyer. (Don't blame the nurseryman; he's just trying to make a living.) If you want the best roses, buy them bare-root from a reliable nursery. I would like to suggest, too, that you take your pail and shovel out into the highways, but I am afraid all you would get nowadays is an oil slick.

Simplify, Simplify

MARK TWAIN ONCE remarked that civilization was a "multiplication of unnecessary necessaries." I believe him; this is one of the reasons I came to the country to live. We have some unnecessary necessaries around here too, just as they do in the cities and suburbs, but not so many. The trouble is, what we think of as luxuries today become necessaries tomorrow. They accumulate like barnacles on a ship's bottom and slow us down just as barnacles do a ship. Pretty soon we are lugging around an accumulation of junk (material and mental) that we have convinced ourselves is needful to our comfort and happiness, when the truth is we got along very well without it before, and would be better off without it today.

I do not exclude myself from this condemnation. As a matter of fact, I can use myself as a case study. The only thing to be said in *my* favor is that I recognize what is happening and am trying—not too successfully—to do something about it. I am not making much headway as far as material possessions are concerned, because I see my attic as merely a magnification of the way my pockets were when I was a kid. Then, my pockets were filled with odd bits of lead for sinkers, twine, colored glass aggies, horse chestnuts, cigarette cards, and on one occasion a live salamander that got me dismissed from class for a while. Now, my attic holds thirty years of *Country Life* magazine (out of which I am going to cut the garden articles some day); fishing tackle I haven't used for a quarter of a century; sails for a boat I no longer own; a box of dress socks, "neelon," as the French lady said who sold them to me; dress shirts yellow with age; old shoes; old hats, straw and Homburg— the list could go on forever. These material things are not the most important; they are, however, evidence of a deeper malaise.

What bothers me, and should concern others living in the Western world during these latter years of the twentieth century, is the importance we have allowed the unnecessaries to assume in our attitude toward life. We really think it is important that we have the latest in color television sets, when in actuality it would make no difference (except we would have more time for useful things) if we had no "telly" at all. We think it critical that our kids get the latest in educational gimmickry, when they—and we—would be better off if they concentrated on learning the basic things at school that they can't get at home. We spend untold millions of dollars on so-called sports, including more money paid to fighters to knock each other silly than has been paid as compensation to all the presidents of our country, back to George Washington.

I have been around for quite a while and I have noticed that the happiest and most contented folk are those who are well-satisfied with the least. I don't minimize the convenience of modern plumbing and the wonders of modern medicine, but even these are magnified far beyond what would be adequate. A bathroom along with every bedroom may be a little more convenient than having to walk down the hall, but it does not prove one is more civilized. In medicine, too, a great deal of time, effort, and money is spent on things that had just as well been left alone. I complained to my physician the other day of some symptoms about which I was mildly apprehensive, and he, instead of ordering a raft of tests, listened and said, "Let's try a little benign neglect," which suited me very well because it is a phrase I am fond of using. I think a little benign neglect would help a lot of things. I mentioned once in an essay a young matron in my church who raised her children on the benign neglect theory, and they were—and are—a couple of the happiest and best-mannered offspring I know.

Our trouble is that we cannot let well enough alone. We are forever wanting to "improve" things, although usually the improvement merely consists of change, whether in cars or weather or lifestyle, which does nothing but sell more cars or complicate the way one lives. The seed man David Burpee, who died not too long ago, spent a lot of money and years of time trying to "create" a white marigold. A more worthless endeavor I cannot conceive. There are plenty of white flowers, the fields are full of them, and marigolds are unsurpassable in their native yellow.

White marigolds in every garden, umpteen bathrooms in every house, a CAT scanner in every hospital, a computer and a color TV in every living room—is this civilization? It is time we listened to Thoreau, who said, "Our life is frittered away by detail. . . . Simplify, simplify."

As Evanescent as a Moonbeam

WHEN I WAS young I had by heart, as the phrase goes, a good deal of poetry. I enjoyed it, and in those far-off days when children were taught many things by rote (the multiplication tables for instance), learning a few verses of poetry day by day fitted nicely into the pattern. Sadly, although I still remember the multiplication tables—to the confusion of cashiers who cannot even add on a calculator—I have forgotten most of the poetry. There are, however, a few lines that remain with me in spite of the years; and among them are those by the English poet Austin Dobson to "A Gentleman of the Old School," which it sometimes pleases me to believe might be me.

Men of a thoughtful and retiring disposition have, since the dawn of civilization, sought the seclusion of the country and extolled the happiness to be found there, far from the hubbub and hurry of urban life. The eighteenth century offers two of our most distinguished citizens as examples. Both Washington and Jefferson wrote many times of shaking off the cares of public office in order to return to Mount Vernon and Monticello, and one can reach back much farther, to the days of Greece and Rome, to listen to Hesiod and Virgil sing the praises of rural life. While I have not read Hesiod for years, there is scarcely a month that I do not turn to the beauty of Virgil's *Georgics* in search of an idea or a half-remembered phrase. But it is of Austin Dobson I am presently thinking.

The swallows came late to Amen Farm this year. The scouts arrived in late May as usual, but the main body was not to be seen volplaning over the tree tops and across the meadow until mid-June, and even then there were fewer birds than in the past. When they failed to arrive in their usual numbers, I told my wife I would have to dig a new pond. I have been filling the old one with garden trash because it always ran dry by late summer, but I now see it held water long enough for the swallows to get mud for their nests. By the time it was dry they were fled south.

What has this to do with Austin Dobson? Well, one of his poems I can still repeat in large part goes as follows:

> HE LIVED SO LONG AGO, YOU SEE!
> MEN WERE UNTRAVELLED THEN BUT WE,
> LIKE ARIEL, POST O'ER LAND AND SEA
>   WITH CARELESS PARTING;
> HE FOUND IT QUITE ENOUGH FOR HIM
> TO SMOKE HIS PIPE IN "GARDEN TRIM"
> AND WATCH, ABOUT THE FISH-TANK'S BRIM,
>   THE SWALLOWS DARTING.

I have no fish-tank, but swallows still dart over the diminished pond, ridding me of blackflies and mosquitoes.

Barn swallows are domestic birds, like robins. They will build their nests in your open garage, or any other structure near your house if you have no barn. I have never seen barn swallows nest far from human habitation. I suppose robins build elsewhere than around houses, but I have never found a robin's nest at Amen Farm very far from a building. There is a robin busy at this moment constructing a nest in an old apple tree not ten feet from where I am writing.

I suppose because I grew up in an old-fashioned garden and in a house with Virgil on the bookshelves, Dobson's nostalgic verses bring back to me the long, endless days of childhood when, if the sun shone, one believed it shone eternally, and if it rained there was no hope it would ever cease. Marcel Proust, in *A la recherche du temps perdu*, speaks of "a long-distant past . . . after the people are dead . . . after the things are broken and scattered . . . smell and taste of things remain . . . in the tiny and almost impalpable drop of their essence, the vast structure of recollection."

But back to Austin Dobson's "Gentleman of the Old School":

HE LIKED THE WELL-WHEEL'S CREAKING TONGUE,—

HE LIKED THE THRUSH THAT FED HER YOUNG,—

HE LIKED THE DRONE OF FLIES AMONG

   HIS NETTED PEACHES;

HE LIKED TO WATCH THE SUNLIGHT FALL

ATHWART HIS IVIED ORCHARD WALL;

OR PAUSE TO CATCH THE CUCKOO'S CALL

   BEYOND THE BEECHES.

Recollections, memory: these are the things that give permanence to living. Without them we have no anchor in the past and no vision of the future, and every moment we live is as evanescent as a moonbeam.

Eggs

THE EGG OF a turkey is about the size of a large hen's egg—say, a double-yolker—but prettier. Its small end is more pointed and the whole egg is attractively speckled with pinkish spots on an off-white background. The shell is harder and the membrane a good bit tougher, so I would guess a turkey poult would have a little more trouble escaping its prison than would the chick of a hen. But from a culinary point of view there is no difference: the eggs look the same, taste the same, and are indistinguishable in the frying pan.

The reason I am so knowledgeable about turkey eggs is this: when we sacrificed our birds to Thanksgiving and Christmas, there were two we had no orders for and no room for in our freezer. Escaping the pogrom were a tom and a hen. They are still in the barn, and the only way I can justify their continued existence in this world is to consider them as pets. From an economic point of view they have long since passed the point of no return, as the value of the grain they have eaten is far in excess of what anyone would pay me for their carcasses. There is, of course, a possibility they might earn their keep for a few more weeks if the hen laid a couple of dozen fertile eggs and then went broody and hatched out some poults with which I could start the new season. However, it is still too cold to let her set even if she showed any signs of doing so—which she has not, and I doubt ever will, for I think it probable all the mothering instincts have been bred out of turkeys, just as they have out of hens. In the meanwhile we enjoy her eggs with our breakfast bacon.

In the days when I commuted fairly regularly to England on business, I was a guest member of a London club that offered gulls' eggs on its menu. You could order them with your drinks if you were so inclined, and I usually was, because they were a novelty to me and were, I thought, very tasty. As I remember them they were about the size of bantams' eggs, but a different color. The shell was bluish and the white was about the same, but the yolk was a bright orange. Gulls' eggs were always served hard-boiled and, and over a couple of drinks, I found I was able to put away several. They cost a shilling apiece then, but I imagine inflation has caught up with the gull's-egg business by now. I mention them not only because the memory is pleasing, but because they had one thing in common with the turkey egg I just had for breakfast: they both had pointed small ends. I am no ornithologist, and I may be wrong, but I think I remember reading that this feature is common to birds' eggs laid on the bare ground or on rocks or a few sticks, where they might roll away if disturbed. (The pointed end acts as a pivot, so the egg just rolls in a circle.) I have never seen a clutch of turkey eggs in the wild so I cannot vouch for them being laid on the ground, but my hen turkey does lay on the floor of the barn—though she might do otherwise if I made a comfortable nest for her.

I don't know what the law is around here about collecting gulls' eggs—and please don't anybody tell me. If I have a fancy for a few eggs I don't want to be scared off by some lawyer. (We have enough trouble with them at Town Meeting—they are always so obstructionist.) Judging from the gulls you have to kick up when you walk across a golf course or a plowed field in England, the eggs collected there seem not to have done anything to diminish their gull population. I understand that in order to be sure of getting fresh eggs the collectors gather and destroy all the eggs in a nest when they begin working in the spring so they can be sure that those they gather daily thereafter are "new laid." I am told the gulls continue to lay for a long time, so the collectors run out of market before the gulls give up. The eggs the English collect are those of the herring gull; whether the eggs of all species of gull are the same, I do not know. I think it remarkable, considering all the garbage gulls eat, that their eggs do not taste fishy or unpleasant, but they do not. But then, chickens on free range will eat anything dead or alive, including each other (dead or alive), and their eggs never vary much in flavor. But I would not want to eat the egg of a shag (cormorant), and I think neither would anyone else who had ever passed to leeward of an island on which they nest.

I notice we have several turkey eggs in the refrigerator, so I think I'll ask my wife to make an omelet of them in the morning. (She makes better omelets than I do.) I am also going to make a note to ask one of my fishermen friends to see what is available in the way of gull eggs on some of the islands. There is still ice in the bay, but the sun is getting higher so even the gulls may be singing

SUMMER IS ICUMEN IN,

LHUDE SING CUCCU!

GROWETH SED, AND BLOWETH MED,

AND SPRINGTH THE WUDE NU—

SING CUCCU!

Beethoven Did Pretty Well

WHEN WE STEPPED outside to bid our dinner guests good night, one of them held up her hand and exclaimed, "Listen! Do you hear the peepers?" Everybody answered yes and there was a "God bless spring" chatter for a few minutes, with someone quoting "the voice of the turtle is heard in our land," which seemed apropos, in conjunction with frogs inhabiting the same surroundings—only the turtle in the Song of Solomon was a turtledove, and not a prospective ingredient of snapper soup.

It being pretty chilly, we did not prolong our farewells, and after we had returned to the warmth of our living room to think about our guests and whether it had been a successful party, I asked Helen, "Could you hear those peepers?" She answered, "Of course, couldn't you?" To which I had to admit I could not. Although I did not say so, I was a little saddened to think I might never listen to the peepers again. I was not distraught, because I can hear most things well enough, and unless I made this confession no one would know my hearing was impaired. However, the world is so filled with the myriad sounds of its breathing that to lose contact with any of them is a grief. I have realized for some time that if I lived long enough I would some- day fail to catch the tintinnabulation of the tinkling temple bells, but the onset of a feared evil always comes as a surprise. Only a few years ago my hearing was keen enough that I could stand by a window and catch the infinitesimal sound of snow rasping against the glass. Today that ability has gone, and the sound of peepers courting has faded with it. Bird song is still with me and so are countless other country signals, loud and soft.

There are, of course, some things I don't mind not hearing: the telephone, for example. I don't do much telephoning, and have never learned the art of socializing on the telephone. When I receive a call, I expect to be asked a question that I can respond to and then hang up; so my wife handles most of our social conversations. She thinks I deliberately fail to hear the ring, but that is not so. (Perhaps we all un- consciously erect a barrier between ourselves and intruders.)

The morning after the party was so heavenly that I went outdoors and sat on a garden seat by our big perennial border, 12 feet wide and 120 feet long, where I was surrounded with daffodils. A song sparrow sang in the tall cedar hedge behind me; a blue jay that could have been heard by the stone-deaf shrieked from the top of the beech tree; there were distant sounds of a lawn mower (as much a symbol of spring as the peepers); and a hen bragged about her personal miracle of having laid an egg. I wonder if every hen is as proud of every egg she lays as a woman is of every baby she brings into the world. It is true eggs come more frequently than babies, but that does not make the event any less a miracle. All life is a miracle—which is the reason warfare is obscene.

As I sat there in the sunshine, a bumblebee landed on a daffodil beside me. It was a big daffodil, a King Alfred, one of those deep yellow fellows with an enormous frilled trumpet, into which the bee disappeared. I could hear him rumbling around at the bottom of the cave, and when he (or she, I am not knowledgeable about the sex of bumblebees) emerged, he staggered through the air in my direction and made a landing on a tiny Johnny-jump-up I had laid on the seat beside me. It seemed ludicrous, this enormous bee on the tiny viola, but it developed that he was not interested in the flower except as something to sit on. He sat there adjusting his collar and tie and brushing his suit, which had become disarranged and covered with pollen during his encounter with the daffodil. He flew around a few times (and I was delighted to discover I could hear his buzzing) and finally, after making a touch-and-go landing on my sleeve, made off toward another clump of daffodils. Watching my friend (he seemed a friend by now), I was reminded of the old aviation story we used to tell, about it being aerodynamically impossible for a bumblebee to fly. He is far too heavy, his wings are too narrow and short, and they move too slowly—but fly he does, nobody having informed him of his limitations.

I can still hear the sea birds calling from where the spring tides wear away at the bluff, at the lower end of our shore pasture, but I don't hear the rote of the sea unless there is a storm of some magnitude. But there, Beethoven got so he couldn't hear a note, and he did pretty well.

SUMMER

Now summer is in flower and natures hum
Is never silent round her sultry bloom
Insects as small as dust are never done
Wi' glittering dance and eeling in the sun
And greenwood fly and blossom haunting bee
Are never weary of their melody.

—*from* The Shepherd's Calendar,
John Clare, 1827

A Countryman

ANYONE WHO IS in the least degree introspective inevitably surveys the events of his past to determine what factors most influenced his character. He wants to know what made him what he is and how he arrived at his position in the world. There may be—and probably are—occurrences and people of enormous importance to us as we go through life, but I believe it is generally accepted that the formative years (say, before fourteen) set the pattern for one's future tastes and behavior, which also means one's success and happiness. My personal belief is that past fourteen years of age the only change that occurs is in intensity: the old man is just the young man magnified. If you are willing to devote a little time to studying someone, anyone you have known long enough, you will inevitably arrive at this conclusion. Perhaps the easiest one to study is yourself, as you know most about yourself. You must, however, keep in mind that you are likely to be prejudiced in your own favor. You are unlikely to have been right as often as you think you were, and more apt to have been less generous and kind than you remember. However, you have all the facts, and an honest analysis will lead you to some interesting conclusions.

If you are a bad sleeper, as I and most other people are as they grow old, the middle of the night is a convenient hour for this exercise. You should keep a scratch pad and a pencil by your bedside and take notes, for ideas that seem quite crystalline at three in the morning often vanish with the rising sun, like the mist in the hollows of the fields. Last night in the mid-watches our little Brittany spaniel discovered she had to go out for a minute, so she blew in my ear, which is her way of getting my attention. In a short while we got back, she to sleep and me to thinking. I decided I would write a piece on the subject I have outlined.

Having lived for a long time, I have met many people; some have swayed my actions but few have had any influence on my beliefs, and almost none have changed my basic preferences. Even though I spent ten years wandering around the world and, subsequently, thirty-five living in cities as a man of business, I am still a countryman. I was born a countryman and measure life against a rural criterion. Had I spent my formative years in a city, my views for the rest of my life would have been colored by that fact. I use country and city as examples because they reflect my own experience, but the principle applies also to other things. If you grow up in a household where music and art surround you and are daily experiences, you will, all your life, differ from a person whose youthful surroundings were dominated by a consuming interest in sports. I do not pass judgment, I merely offer it as something to remember.

Apart from my rural background, I know very well that my love of books, beginning when I was about six, has intensified all my life and has been a major factor in determining what I have accomplished and what I have engaged in. I do love books just for themselves, but I am not a collector. My library reflects my personal interests. A professional librarian would not consider mine a very good assortment, as it is too specialized, but I enjoy my books and read them and use them, and I would find life very drab without them.

I have a great affection for librarians. In balance with the amount of good they do, they are the most underpaid people in our society. I do not refer now to the guardians of places on the scale of the Library of Congress, but to the ladies—and I use the word advisedly—who sit behind desks in the thousands of small libraries scattered across the length and breadth of the country. Librarians, even more than teachers, have an enormous influence on the young. Librarians can guide young people along paths denied the teacher, who has to concentrate on the subjects being taught. The librarian is able to send the inquiring mind off the beaten paths and into fields of sheer delight. It was my village librarian who introduced me to Kenneth Grahame's *Wind in the Willows*. (If she had never done another thing she should have been canonized for that.) I learned about Rat, and Mr. Toad, and Mr. Badger, and "Dulce domum," which was also my school song; now, more than eighty years later, it seems impossible that *The Wind in the Willows* has not been a classic forever. Well, I suppose for most people it has, but in 1908, when my friendly librarian put it in my way, it had just been published.

And so I come back to the beginning of this essay, in which I set forth as a theorem that a man is molded into shape before he has hair on his upper lip (you can choose your own simile for girls); I invite you to pursue the subject further during your next sleepless night.

A Countryman's Farewell

Zumbadores

NANCY JUST CAME into the room where my wife and I were drinking our morning coffee, with a hummingbird in her hand. It was dead, but the ruby ruff around its neck was still iridescent and its beady eyes were not yet filmed over. She had found it on the ground outside the kitchen door. There were no marks of injury and one would suppose it had flown into a window, except that I have never known a hummingbird to do that. Other birds do, but in my experience not hummers. I have watched them cruise along a sheet of glass just about two inches from it, never varying their distance. I suppose the reason is that their wings, which vibrate at from thirty to seventy-five beats a second, set up an area around them like a magnetic field so they can feel the proximity of something before they touch it, even if it is invisible, just as bats are able to avoid objects in the dark.

Hummingbirds arrive at Amen Farm about two weeks after the barn swallows, which means they don't get here until the middle of May, but they stay until October whereas the swallows leave in August. We have a late garden—with the added attraction of color in the greenhouse, which hummingbirds fly in and out of to suit the occasion—so they stay with us even into November in mild seasons. I found one in the greenhouse this morning. There are red flowers there—geraniums and fuchsias mainly—which hummers seem to prefer. (Outdoors at this time of year, yellows predominate.) The bird was dipping into the blossoms, but when it saw me it decided to leave. It didn't panic but just wandered along the glass looking for an exit. I watched it for several minutes as it stood still in the air and then drifted up and down and sideways like a helicopter, puzzled by the invisible barrier. Eventually I opened the door and it soon found its way out.

Although there are approximately five hundred species of hummingbirds, only the ruby-throated is ever seen in New England. This is our smallest bird and probably the most agile and pugnacious. It is helped in its battles by its extraordinary ability to fly backward. I have only once seen a hummingbird's nest. It was built rather far out on the branch of an elm tree and swayed with every breeze. That same summer I was lucky enough to witness hummingbird courting procedure. The lady sat on a twig while her suitor swung in arcs before her like a jewel in the sunlight.

Hummingbirds are plentiful around here; all one has to do to attract them to a garden is to grow plenty of flowers, preferably red, although they are catholic in their tastes and will try anything. Even though they spend so much time honey-dipping, hummingbirds are said to also feed on small insects, which I suppose they find in the flowers. About the only way to verify this would be to catch one and analyze the contents of its stomach, an enterprise I am not about to get into.

Some years ago while I was in Mexico, I was fortunate enough to be able to buy a copy of a book, beautifully illustrated, by an artist named Montes de Oca, entitled *Hummingbirds and Orchids of Mexico*. It had been printed in Germany in two editions of five hundred, one in Spanish and the other in English. If you are within reach of a large library you might find a copy there, and I am sure you would enjoy looking at it. As this is primarily a picture book it doesn't matter whether you see the Spanish or English version.

Hummingbirds and Orchids of Mexico has an interesting history. The original watercolors were painted more than a hundred years ago, but the artist was unable to interest anyone in reproducing them, so they remained in the possession of the family of one of his pupils until eventually they were published in 1963. It was suggested many times that the collection be broken up and framed individually or pasted on a screen, which would have been the end of them. Fortunately the elderly lady who owned the watercolors would have none of it, so we have her to thank for the enjoyment we get from them today.

From de Oca's book I learned that the names of hummingbirds, regardless of language, are almost always onomatopoetic, that is to say, imitative of a sound associated with the thing being described. In Spanish they are *zumbadores*, in French *bourdonneurs*, and in English hummingbirds, *humming* being another onomatopoetic word. But it is the old indigenous languages of Latin America that provide the most delightful examples: in Tarascan the name is *tzintzun*, in Mayan *dzunuun*, in Nahuatl *uitzitzilin*. In the Spanish of Colombia they are *runrunes*, in Cuba *zunzunes*. Though not onomatopoetic, some of their other names in Latin America, derived from their association with flowers, are beguiling: *chupaflor*, *chuparrosa*, *chupamirto*, and *picaflor* for instance, and in Portuguese *beija-flor* (flower-kisser).

Next time you see a *zumbadora*, whistle "tzintzun" to it; maybe it will mistake you for a flower.

Me and My Body

A VISITOR WHO came looking for me the other day was told I could be found in the Japanese garden. It is, I think, a pretty garden, but the only thing Japanese about it is the presence of a stone lantern and a number of large boulders—honest Maine boulders, which are probably like boulders in Japan. When my caller pushed through the little white gate in the stone wall that partially surrounds the garden he was astonished to find me lying, like Goya's Maja (only with more clothes on), alongside a planting of heather out of which I was trying to winkle some weeds. As the years have passed I have learned there are two ways I can work comfortably in the garden: one is upright behind a hoe, which is destructive in a small flower bed, and the other is prone with my face close to the weeds. It is not that I need to be there to see what I am doing, as my eyesight is excellent. I am sure of that because the state just renewed my driver's license without restriction. However, bending is difficult and so is kneeling, a position where Kipling said a proper gardener spent half his life. So, it is either up or down for me.

After deciding I had not suffered a heart attack or a stroke ("shock" we call it in Maine) my guest was obviously relieved, but he asked anyway, as an opening gambit, "How are you?" To which I replied, "If you will go over there and sit on that bench and wait a few minutes until I get my body into a vertical position, I'll come and tell you." He did, and I did.

What I told him was that like most people, he was confusing me with my body. I reminded him of the story of John Quincy Adams, who in extreme old age told an inquirer after his health that he, Adams, was fine but the tenement he occupied was in bad shape. The roof leaked, the foundations were shaky, et cetera, and if things did not soon improve he was going to have to vacate and find lodgings elsewhere. Most people fall into my visitor's error. They think that because troubles develop with a person's physical equipment, something ails him. Nothing could be farther from the truth. A man's body is just the place he occupies, like Mr. Adams's tenement. True, if something goes wrong with his body he has difficulty in making it behave as he was able to do when it was in order, but that does not mean that *he* is any different.

People often tell me I look younger than I am, which used to flatter me but no longer does, because all it means is that they expect more of my body than it can deliver. I tell them, "Yes, the paint job is standing up very well, but don't look under the hood. The valves are leaky, the springs are rusty, and the shock absorbers are a disaster. These things, however, bother others much more than they do me, so don't fash yourself."

I don't know much about theology, but I have a notion that most religions teach this division between what they call the soul and the body. The trouble is, they make it all so mysterious that it is detached from everyday life. I don't think of me, my soul, or spirit, or inner self, or whatever else you want to call it, as being on an ethereal plane. It is right here now with its hand on the throttle. Its obvious first job is to keep its physical plant in as good shape as possible, which does not have to mean devoting all its time to thinking about it, chomping granola or drinking buttermilk or swallowing vitamins. What it does mean is that we should endeavor to maintain an equilibrium, realizing that no matter what develops we must in the final analysis work with what we have.

If you are ill or handicapped through old age or otherwise (it doesn't have to be old age, you know; plenty of people who are quite young have less that perfect access to the world because their tenement is shaky) the happiest course is to do what you can and enjoy what is around. Plenty of people do. I'd rather bend over to a weed, but if I have to lie down, so be it. I am closer to "the good earth" anyway—and having viewed a good many plump gardeners from behind while they were weeding, I am sure my way is a lot more graceful.

Naskeag

THE FOG THAT has beset us for the last several days has thinned, leaving a vaporous silver haze. Misty clouds hang over the off-shore islands, Gott and Little Gott, Swans, and the others, making them appear much higher than they are, almost mountainous. I rode to the harbor, and standing on the shore could see under the lifting mist. No one else was there, for Naskeag Harbor is a working harbor little frequented by summer people and their pleasure craft, and the lobstermen and clammers had long gone. I hear the fishermen driving by my house at the first light, often earlier, for their days start when the rest of us are still sleeping. When, on rare occasions, I have had to be about before dawn, perhaps when starting out on a trip, I have seen lights in the kitchens of all the fishermen's houses as they eat breakfast and fix their lunch pails.

I am fortunate to live in such peace. Not everybody would think so, I admit, but I enjoy the wide margin it gives my life. We have visitors, who after a few days, much as they say they enjoy the quiet, soon yearn for the crowds and bustle of the cities and their suburbs.

Naskeag Point (I live about three miles down the road to the harbor) is five miles long and about a mile wide. When I listen to the weather report I wait for the marine forecast, for living here is like being on a ship or an island. Frequently the sun will be shining in the village while fog still embraces us on the Point. This marine weather keeps us cooler in the summer and warmer in the winter, for the ocean acts as a vast air-conditioner. It does, that is, except when it freezes—but that rarely happens. In all the years I have lived here, only a couple of times have I seen the bay frozen the whole six or seven miles to Mount Desert Island. Even then it was not frozen solid enough for one to walk across, as there were leads and small patches of blue water where the ebb and flow of the tide kept the ice broken and in motion. But a bay that is even 90 percent ice does not have much of an ameliorating effect on the weather. Shorter distances have been negotiable by boys on snowmobiles, who have made the one-mile trip to Long Island, and one winter a man and his sons walked to Hog Island, leaving little spruce branches stuck in holes they chopped in the ice to mark their passage, but generally saltwater ice is unreliable.

There is no ice today, though. Great mounds of wild pink roses billow along the roadsides, distilling their fragrance for the pleasure of the passer-by. The plumy goldenrod begins to show chartreuse on its tips as it sways in the gentle breeze. Here and there a clump of tawny day lilies mark where there was once a house—or perhaps only where someone discarded some garden rubbish containing a few roots that took hold. Perhaps day lilies learned to hang on so tenaciously to life in their native China, where existence for common people has never been easy. Lilacs, too, live on long after the houses beside whose doors they were planted have crumbled into their cellar holes, but the lilacs bloomed earlier and are now resting and gathering strength for another spring.

I have a map of Brooklin that shows all the houses on Naskeag Point in 1881, including mine. The map shows about thirty-five buildings, and I doubt there are any more than fifty now. Hardly a population explosion, and of course some of today's houses are owned by summer residents, which was not the case when the map was drawn. I am sure a man from 1881 would have no difficulty with his surroundings if he were to be reincarnated here today, and in some houses he would find his descendants still living.

The Town of Brooklin was incorporated in 1849 but is much older, having been a part of Sedgwick, which was founded in 1789. Actually there were people living on Naskeag Point long before then. A man named Shadrach Watson (who had his little day of glory when the town was called Port Watson for a year) ran a store on Naskeag Point as early as 1762, and there had to be others to whom he sold his goods. It is also recorded that a French family lived here in the late 1600s, so our point has had a resident population for many years. Happily, it has never grown much, and we hope it never does. The Indians who used to summer here, fishing and clamming, left in the winter just as "summer people" do now. When the traffic thins out in a few weeks life here will be much as it has always been. The wild roses and goldenrod will be gone, but the maples will catch fire, and the leaves will fall from the birches so I can once more enjoy an uninterrupted view of the bay.

Long, Empty Roads

A LOT OF PEOPLE promise to visit me while they are on vacation, and a few actually do, but many more find Amen Farm farther from U.S. Route 1 than they anticipated. Only the more courageous visitor to Maine strays far from Route 1. Some do take a chance—and then get lost or find they have run out of time. More are kept from adventuring by the magic of the name Bar Harbor and the familiar signs of the national motels and the fast-food stops they are accustomed to further south. The empty roads leading from Route 1 down the long peninsulas that make up Maine's coastline create apprehension in the minds of drivers who have not been out of sight of other cars since they crossed the border at Kittery.

Ours is a large state—nearly as big as all the rest of New England put together—and once you get away from the few principal highways you can drive for miles between villages, or even before you glimpse an occasional house half-hidden in the woods. Where I live, on the coast, the population is more concentrated than it is further inland, but even so the miles stretch out. Naskeag Point, by the most direct route, is thirty miles from Route 1, and if shortly after leaving Bucksport you spy a sign pointing to Route 175 and take it, saying to yourself "Aha! That is the road," you will drive fifty miles before you reach us because you will be on the wrong end of the route.

The reason for the empty roads inland is easily understood: it is just that there is a very small population and a vast amount of land. On the coast it is because until the 1920s the area enjoyed a dependable steamboat service (the last regular steamboat service to Brooklin ended in 1934), and the centers of population for the most part were concentrated on navigable waters. Studying a map of Maine, you will find few towns that are not on rivers or tidewater. Small villages like my own enjoyed excellent service by sail and steam long before they had year-round roads, but public transportation on land we never had. Railroads, for the most part, except for the narrow-gauge carriers, operated only between the largest cities—and as for the interurban trolleys that were such a vogue in much of the country, we had few urban districts for them to be "inter." I learned, when I lived in Sullivan Harbor, that in the lifetime of a neighbor no older than I, the mails east of Ellsworth were carried by stagecoach.

Our few industries, except for shipbuilding and paper, do not call for concentrations of workers. While these facts distress people who feel civilization is measured by industrial development and a growing population, and that to be happy and fulfilled one must have more material things each succeeding year than one had the year before, the truth is that our widely dispersed population is infinitely better-off and happier than those living in more sophisticated surroundings. They may not be as well-off financially, but wealth depends upon many more things than the size of one's pay envelope. How you spend what you have has a lot to do with it. What we do have in Maine, and what is constantly attracting more people to the state, is a stable society with little crime and a love of place that it is now hard to find elsewhere. Stability is the key word. Our town, and small towns like it along the coast, are still populated to a surprising degree by descendants of the families who settled here two hundred years ago. True, some of the young leave to secure employment elsewhere, but many return bringing new skills with them, and many who stay away return after retirement. In a city or its suburbs new residents are swallowed by an amorphous body without character; here they remain individuals. It is a canard that the members of old established families reject newcomers; they merely wait to see how the newcomers are going to behave before making a judgment of them, which seems to me a reasonable attitude.

Those long empty roads are our protection against the trivial. If someone really wants to come here he can find the way, and if he enjoys the country and small villages and is willing to keep quiet and not make waves for a few years, he will find a people and a way of life rewarding beyond measure.

Continuity

I SUPPOSE MOST readers past middle age (whenever that may be) can remember how on some appropriate occasion—a birthday, the Fourth of July, or Christmas Day perhaps—the children of the family would be stood up against a doorjamb and lines would be drawn on it to record their heights. Everyone's door casings carried such historical markings, with the date and subject's name recorded for posterity to reflect upon. If a family had lived in a house for several generations (which more often than not was the case in those days), one could compare Grandfather's altitude at a certain age with that of succeeding generations. Such evidence was available in the house in which I grew up, and I was so fortunate as to have a grandfather who could point out to me his father's memorial as well as his own. The house is gone now, as are all those who contributed to its history, except me. I am sorry. It would have been pleasant to have added my great-grandchildren's marks to the collection.

There may be a few families where the custom still prevails, but they must be rare, for nowadays not many people live in the houses in which their fathers or mothers grew to maturity. Currently, a mark of success seems to be the acquisition of a new and larger house every few years, a habit that automatically rules out the possibility of one's home ever becoming so intertwined with one's life that it carries within it a record of its old inhabitants. We are also now a mobile society—many of us are, anyway—so the house we live in is of no particular importance other than that it must be comfortable and as large and up-to-date as our ability to carry the mortgage permits. Even so, there must be, here and there, people who watch their kids grow taller inch by inch and keep records on the woodwork, though most just have the records kept by the pediatrician on his scorecard.

All of the visible wood in the house I grew up in was unpainted oak, so that a few scorelines and some scribbling did not show much, and anyway people were not so fussy as they are today. They did not paint the insides of their houses so often. (I painted the inside of my home here in Maine thirty years ago and it is unlikely I shall do it again.) Your modern housewife wants to be up-to-date with interior decorating trends and is apt to do over the whole inside of the house any time she gets tired of the old paint job, so it is unlikely that future generations will be able to examine the early records of their forebears' growth. I suppose all this is inevitable, what with the population explosion and everybody wanting their own new house, but I think it a bit sad. There is a great deal to be said for family history, even if it is only marks on a doorjamb.

I was lucky enough to have been born quite a long time ago,

when most country people were part of a continuum. They were not just dumped "on the shore of the wide world . . . alone and palely loitering," like the knight-at-arms in *La belle dame sans merci*. They were like an eye or an arm or a foot, a part of the greater whole. That this was not true of the poor devils born and raised in the slums of industrial cities I know full well, but, sadly, the world has never been perfect and is never likely to be. At least the rural population was a segment of something greater than its individual parts. People planned more for the future because they believed there would be a future. Houses and farms stayed in the family, and young men continued the trades or professions of their fathers. There was a feeling of calm. Truly, home was a place to which you could always return when you could go nowhere else. People understood the parable of the Prodigal Son.

A custom in England, where I grew up, was for the father, upon the birth of a son, to buy a case or two of port wine if he was rich (or a bottle or two if he was only modestly endowed) and set it aside to be opened on his son's twenty-first birthday. It didn't cost much, but was a statement of confidence in the future. It might be a good custom for us to revive now, in 1988. Even if you move half a dozen times between now and 2009, you can take your port with you, and, with luck, 2009 will be a good year to celebrate. If it is not, and is as bad as the pessimists predict, then the port will serve to drown your sorrow.

If you don't drink port, I am sorry for you, very sorry, but I have an alternative suggestion: you could plant a tree when your son is born. True, as the poet says, only God can make a tree, but anybody can plant one. It is not likely that you will be able to take it with you if you move, but it will always give pleasure to someone, and that, in a way, is projecting your life into the future.

Bears

A FEW DAYS AGO my wife received a telephone call from a neighbor, who complained in a somewhat aggrieved tone that there was a bear in her dooryard. It was not doing anything, just standing there looking very large. She and her husband were both indoors and, I judge, had no artillery around. She wanted suggestions as to what to do. Helen asked if she should send Ivar along to survey the situation, and the offer was accepted.

Ivar, who does most anything around here, borrowed my scope-equipped .243 (not a heavy-caliber rifle, but a deadly weapon that will in the right hands pick a fly off a post at a hundred yards), and set off in our truck to rescue the damsel in distress. When he arrived, the bear—a big black three-hundred-pounder—was standing on all fours in the driveway, appreciating the springtime.

When young Lochinvar returned I asked, "Did you shoot it?" and he had to admit rather sheepishly that he had not fired a shot. He had forgotten to load the gun before he left, and by the time he had performed that useful and necessary act the bear had ambled off into the woods. Anyway, the law says you must not carry a loaded gun in the car, so he had an out. I believe my neighbors stayed pretty close to home for the rest of the day.

We don't have many bears around here; you hear of, or see, about one a year on average. When they do show up it is usually in the spring. I suppose she-bears go cruising for food for their cubs, or maybe the wanderlust of the vernal days gets into the veins of any bear, regardless of sex. I don't believe they are particularly dangerous, although I wouldn't want to wrestle one. A smaller specimen than our current bear was seen in Brooksville a couple of weeks ago, where it killed a pig—or three pigs, depending on whose story you heard—so my concern was for my lambs, which are only a few weeks old and would make tasty hors d'oeuvres for a bear.

The next time I heard about Bruin was when I received advice that it had been seen wandering down the road in front of the old poor-farm. Subsequently it was reported standing on the porch of a local taxpayer's house, eating out of the bird feeder. Somebody called the game warden to complain about the theft, and the only response he got from Rolly was that bears have to eat, too. Come to think of it, they do.

Having lived in Maine a long time, I have seen quite a few bears. Some I saw fortuitously; others I went looking for. I have a notion that bears have no more wish to meet you than you have to meet them. You are not likely to find bears by walking around in the woods, and if you do, these are the fortuitous sightings. Only once have I seen a bear in the woods. I was staying at Grant's Camps on Lake Kennebago and had been studying a map of the area, which showed a delightful small pond about two miles away over a low ridge that was reachable by a rough trail. I made the hike and found that the pond was indeed beautiful, but only about a foot or so deep. There were a million trout in it, but they were minnows; the pond was a natural hatchery.

On my way back to camp, armed only with a three-ounce fly rod, I stopped at an open spot on the ridge to pick a handful of raspberries. When I stood up, there was my bear, about a hundred feet away. He heard me, and stood up to get a better look. He was about as big as the Abominable Snowman and looked to me to weigh a thousand pounds. I left hastily, and when I snapped a quick glance over my shoulder to see if he was following, what I saw was his rear end as he galumphed off into the bushes.

Fishermen have a notion that the earlier they get up in the morning, the more fish they will catch. The "cookee" at Grant's got up to light his fires about five o'clock, and if you wanted a cup of coffee and a doughnut before you went trout-hunting, you could get the provender by visiting his kitchen. Like most camps, Grant's kept a couple of live garbage-disposals, which started off small but were sizable porkers by fall. While you were drinking your coffee you could watch the pigs sharing their swill with the bears. At least you could until the moment Cookee saw them too and, with profanity and dire maledictions, took out after the bears with a long-handled iron skillet. These were the bears you could look for and find.

One morning last year as Ivar rounded the corner by our barn, a bear fell down the bank in front of the truck. It bounced off the fender unhurt, except for losing a little hair, and disappeared into the woods. Ivar and a young fellow who was with him went after it and fortunately were unsuccessful in their search. I am glad it escaped unharmed.

Of all animals, man is the most murderous. His immediate reaction when he sees anything wild is to kill it. He has conditioned himself, with great effort, not to routinely kill other men, but periodically, when he can't hold back any longer, he calls a moratorium on peace and slaughters his fellows by the millions. Sometimes he can't even wait for a war, but cooks up some excuse or other and murders three or four million Jews or a million-and-a-half Armenians just for the hell of it.

I'm glad our bear left town. Every man's hand was against it. It probably won't be much better off wherever it goes, but its blood won't be on my head.

Foxes

ALTHOUGH I HAVE owned this smallish patch of land on the Maine coast for over thirty years, I did not do much about making a garden until I came here to live full time twenty-six years ago. The years before then I spent scurrying around the world trying to earn enough money to stay here. By 1962 I decided I had reached that goal and thought I had better settle down (after all, one does not expect to live forever), so I settled, convincing all my urban friends I was out of my mind, when they had only suspected it before.

Amen Farm covers about eighty acres (more or less, as the deed hedges), which suburbanites might not consider a smallish patch of land, but all things are relative. Maine has an area of 33,215 square *miles*, and since an acre is but $\frac{1}{640}$th of a square mile, a little arithmetic will suggest I am not a land baron. I might add also, to diminish further the importance of my property, that it resembles a farm my father once owned that he said was half rocks and half trees. He complained that the Creator had gone off before he finished the job. If God had put all the trees on half the land, and all the rocks on the other half, it would have saved Father a lot of work. Amen Farm was like that when the first owner arrived 128 years ago, and I have him to thank for clearing about ten acres to provide room for a house and a hayfield. Wanting a pasture for my few cattle, I cleared another four acres, and even though I did it with a bulldozer, I got some notion of what my predecessor had been up against. The windrow of glacial boulders from my operation still stretches like the fallen walls of Jericho across the bottom of the pasture, providing luxurious lodgings for my resident foxes, who yesterday killed and dragged away two turkeys.

When I said it would be too bad if someone shot the bear (or bears) that have been wandering around here, I was not personally involved. They were not my pigs the bear had eaten, so I could afford to be forgiving. I might have felt differently if the bear had eaten one of my lambs (which I planned on eating myself) but it didn't; so, as I said, I bore it no ill will. But, thanks to my English childhood, I was brought up to believe that a man who shot a fox was morally on a par with a thief who stole the communion silver from an altar. True, you fenced foxes out of your henhouse, but if foxes broke in or picked up a couple of your free-range pullets you didn't pull a gun on them. All you had to do to be compensated was to carry your complaint to the master of the local hunt. Anyway, if you were a farmer you probably rode with the hunt yourself.

Just to see a fox gives a lift to the spirit. I think of all animals they are the most graceful, even more so than deer. Foxes don't run, they just flow over the ground, like the wind fondling a field of grain. When I lived in Pennsylvania, the nearest hunt kennels were on a hill about three miles away across a little valley. Whenever I heard the baying of the hounds I knew the hunt would soon come galloping down the opposite hill and that in a short while I would see the fox, which usually followed the same route over my land. In the middle of one of my fields was an enormous pile of brush where the fox would take cover when hard-pressed. I never burned the brush, and I am sure the hunt was happy I did not, even though many of their foxes went to ground there. However, at the time, I didn't have any hens to worry about.

When I looked out of my bedroom window yesterday morning I saw a fox cover the last fifty yards to the fence and go under it. The creature was in beautiful condition with a large bushy tail, and when Ivar with his gun came running along the fence a second later, I was happy that he was too late. The sheep were huddled together alongside a large field boulder but the fox took no notice of them. It was too interested in my turkeys, and I doubt would have attacked a flock of sheep anyway.

I guess I never did get back to that pasture I started off writing about, but that is the trouble with living in the country—there is always something to toll you away from your job. If it isn't a bear it's a fox, or the deer that have eaten most of the buds off the azaleas, or perhaps the visitors I complain about but secretly love because they give me an opportunity to show off my flowers and avoid for a few minutes the work I should be doing.

The Other Natives

WHILE COMPARED TO most people living in the eastern part of the country we in Maine live in a sparsely populated area, we are not in really wild territory. True, Maine is the most heavily forested state in the nation: more than 87 percent woodland (2.5 million acres of which you should not enter without a guide)—but the fact is, most of the population live in a wide strip along the coast. Even there, though, except around a few "big" cities—Portland (sixty-one thousand), Lewiston (forty thousand), and Bangor (thirty-one thousand)—you can be in the country in twenty minutes, so man has not made much impression on the native nonhuman population. We coexist.

I had this fact brought to my mind by the sight of dead trees, swamped because of the recent construction of a couple of beaver dams. Both dams are alongside the road where the traveller cannot help seeing them, so goodness knows how many there are where they cannot be so easily observed. The dam I pass every day is between my house and the village, practically in my back yard, and the other I observe every time I drive to Blue Hill. The one on the Naskeag Road is a considerable annoyance to our selectmen, because the busy little beavers insist on plugging up a culvert that runs under the road, with consequences I leave to your imagination. The one in South Blue Hill presents less of a problem because it has been built as a small replica of the Grand Coulee Dam, a little upstream from the culvert, with its height such that excess water flows around the ends of the dam. It is a beautiful structure, with grass now growing along the top, and is, I am sure, solid enough to be walked on. Upstream, flooding from the dam has killed the alders along the banks and has spread to swamp out firs and spruces farther back. It does not take much standing water over their roots to kill trees and shrubs, just a few inches will do it, and as soon as the flood gets above a stream bank it will quickly cover several acres of level land. I believe the Blue Hill beavers are still in residence, but the game warden has trapped several of those on the Naskeag Road and lugged them off to wilder surroundings. This is, however, only a temporary expedient because new visitors, enchanted with what we have to offer, will soon replace them.

People coming from city or suburb, seeing our paved roads, mail delivery, library, church, store, and other signs of civilization, equate our surroundings with their own. They are not the same. When I tell our guests not to be alarmed if they hear noises in the night outside their guest cottage—that it is much more likely to be a bear than a robber—they look at me in disbelief, but what I say is true. Maine is a safe place to live (it ranks as low as forty-eighth of the fifty states in the frequency of violent crime), but we do have living with us, cheek by jowl, almost everything that walks, crawls, or flies and is natural to the climate. One is led astray because, commonly, these are not seen.

Gilbert White relates that "a very intelligent Gentleman" assured him that "the mean rain of any place cannot be ascertained till a person has measured it for many years . . . He speaks from upwards of 40 years experience." This same observation could justly be made about the presence of our wild neighbors, many of whom, in spite of their constant presence, one sees only occasionally. I have lived in Brooklin since 1957, and have seen just about everything on wings or feet that lives here—but if I had made my home here for only twenty-eight years instead of thirty one, I would not have seen beavers, though they have been resident the whole time.

When I first arrived, before I had really settled in and the workmen were still trying to make my house habitable, I looked out of the window one morning—and there, to my amazement, was a moose trampling down the seedlings in my vegetable garden. Everyone knows, or is told, that moose are so plentiful in northern Maine that they need to be culled (a polite word for killed) in order to maintain the vigor of the herd. Nonetheless, one does not look for them on the coast. Personally I have never again seen one, though rarely a year passes without a report of a moose being in town.

Deer, which arouse the hunting instinct in almost everybody but me (I am too old, and don't like venison except for the liver anyway), are a nuisance. We don't see them in the summer, but come fall and winter they spend their time browsing on my best evergreens. One thing they love is yew—*Taxus*, any species, the rarer the better. I was taught as a boy that yew was deadly to horses, but I can affirm without fear of contradiction that deer—which must be blood brothers to goats—eat it with impunity. We have to build an enclosure around two large yew at our front entrance every winter. Even more expensive is the electric fence we have to erect around the woods garden where the azaleas live. There are acres of cedars nearby, which are a deer's natural winter browse, but they prefer to nip the flower buds out of the azaleas. An hors d'oeuvre, I suppose.

One day my wife and I were driving home, and seeing a school bus coming toward us at the edge of the village, we braked to a halt. The bus discharged a couple of kids and we moved ahead. To our surprise and delight, not more than a hundred feet farther on, a large bobcat came out of the bushes and walked unhurriedly across the road. Its bobbed tail and clipped ears were unmistakable, and it was obviously not scared of anything. I heard later that somebody had lost a few hens and had called for the game warden to do some shooting, but so far as I know the sinner went free.

Once on a winter night with snow on the ground, we were driving home late from a dinner party, and as we came through Blue Hill Village with neither people nor cars in sight and only a few lights, a slender form fled across the road in front of us. It seemed to have no legs and was the color of the snow—all but the tip of its tail, which was black. A weasel, of course, and all arrayed in its royal clothing of ermine. I have only seen three weasels since I came here to live, but there must be thousands. One of the other two sightings was in our guest house, where we found one dead under a chest; the third was very much alive, running over my foot in pursuit of a chipmunk that sought refuge in the stone wall beside which I was standing. (I didn't see the rest of the play, but I would not have wanted to be the chipmunk because the interstices of a dry stone wall are no place to hide from a weasel.)

We have small creatures a-plenty, though I see fewer since our old cat, Butterscotch, left us for, I hope, a better world (although I must add that like most of us Butterscotch seemed well-satisfied with this one). She regularly presented me with her catch (bragging, of course), which might range from something as small as a shrew up to a snowshoe hare she could barely drag along. Chipmunks, red squirrels, mice of varying species, birds from robins to hummers—all were exhibited. Among the exotica were a bat (species unknown), a flying squirrel, and, most interesting to me, a mouse that I am sure I never saw before. As it seemed unharmed I stole it from her, and while my wife held Butterscotch, placed the mouse on the ground. After a moment's pause to overcome its previous hypnotic state, with one prodigious leap, the mouse was away in the tall grass. Perhaps it was a kangaroo mouse, though my books do not tell me if that species is native to Maine.

I have said nothing about my sworn enemies, the raccoons, which I usually refer to as "those damn coons." I have never seen a raccoon in all the time I have lived in Maine, except for ones crossing the road (or a tame one), but during the years I tried to grow corn, raccoons unfailingly stole all my crop just as it got ripe. I tried fences, electric wires, radios, lights, strips of foil, and traps, but all I ever succeeded in doing was catching Butterscotch (who was understandably annoyed with me) and a couple of skunks. I don't mind skunks; I see *them* frequently and we never bother each other. Where skunks are concerned, live and let live is our motto, but a skunk in a Have-a-Heart trap is a problem. All I can recommend is that you turn the job of releasing it over to someone you out-rank.

Twice recently I have seen the corpse of an opossum beside the road. I had not realized they could be found so far north, always thinking of them as a dainty dish enjoyed by Southern blacks. (I was encouraged in that belief by a gardener who helped me around my place in New London, Pennsylvania. His name was Rochester, and he claimed "possum" was "good eatin'," but I never tried one and don't think they are abundant enough here for the opportunity to present itself.

I haven't said anything yet about the porcupines that ravish my rowan trees and poplars every spring. They climb the trees and cut off lighter branches, which litter the ground, but they do not seem to eat them. Until I fenced in my kitchen garden, porcupines got fat on whatever I happened to plant. I did not fence in the garden so much in order to save the vegetables as to avoid getting apoplexy. There used to be a bounty on porcupines (you had to present the game warden with the feet to collect it), but there is no bounty now, and there seem to be neither fewer nor more porcupine feet than before. I have written before about a school teacher I once knew who was death on porcupines. Armed with a two-by-three that had one end whittled into a handle to provide a ladylike grip, she had no trouble in catching up with a garden-bound porky and hitting it on the nose—its only vulnerable spot—with her cudgel. She would then turn it over and cut out its liver with a paring knife. (I later gave her a more deadly and somewhat larger weapon.) She'd eat the liver for breakfast. Being curious, I tried it once, with one of our resident porkies as the donor. But I'd rather have chicken liver, which I can obtain more easily in the supermarket.

This winter I have been bothered by red squirrels. I do see *them* every day. They are attractive at a distance, and I don't mind contributing to their welfare—they eat more sunflower seed than all the birds around—but they are as destructive as rats, or more so, if they get in your house. This winter a squirrel genius climbed our old lilac, got into the gutter, and gnawed a hole under the overhang of the shingles, thus gaining entrance to the attic. There being nothing there to eat, it scrambled down between the studding and gnawed another hole into the shed so it and its relatives could help themselves to the bird seed we store there. We decided that action was called for, so reluctantly shot all the squirrels that showed up for a week. It made not the least impression. Every day there were three or four more. We were defeated. We mended the hole under the eaves and prayed for spring, when the squirrels would return to the woods. I said something to Ivar about squirrel pie, but a red squirrel minus skin wouldn't even feed a squirrel.

The Most Comforting Spot

R ICHARD L. STROUT, whose column in the *Christian Science Monitor* I see occasionally, wrote a piece in the September 5, 1980, issue entitled "The Most Comforting Spot in All America." If you haven't read it and have access to that issue of the paper through your library or elsewhere, I suggest you give it a few minutes of your time. The title tells it all. Specifically, it is about a small town in New Hampshire, a man's family, and where and how they lived for five generations. It is not big news. The town hasn't much notable history except that His Majesty's timber surveyors used to snake masts out of the local woods for the Royal Navy in the years before the Revolution. However, like a fish swimming into chum, you soon find yourself snatching at thoughts that remind you of what was to you the "most comforting spot in all America." In years past we were all able to recall places like that, but nowadays it is different. If you are born in a hospital delivery room, grow up in a city with both parents working, and move frequently, there is not much of anywhere for that second (let alone the fifth) generation to return to, either physically or in memory.

I was not born in a city, nor in a hospital either, but even so I have no slightest recollection of the place where I was born, because I left there as an infant and never returned. I know it was in the country, and I am pretty sure the event did not make much of a splash, so I cannot, like Richard Strout, find comfort in the place of my birth. Had I grown up there, it might have been different, but when I was a small boy of five I was sent to England to be brought up by my grandparents. (How does the old saw go—seven years baby, seven years boy, seven years hobbledehoy.) When I graduated to manhood I wandered off again, and though in my mature years I lived for half a lifetime near a big Eastern city, I never found the "most comforting spot in all America."

My childhood and adolescent recollections are of my maternal grandfather's house, where his family had lived for many more than five generations. However, I was not born there, an omission for which my grandfather never forgave my mother. That ancient house, now long gone, is no more than a fugitive memory—like that of the first girl I ever kissed. I will never forget her but I can never see her again. I can re-create in my mind's eye that old dwelling, but like that first kiss, it has suffered a sea-change into the stuff that dreams are made on. It is not a comfort to which I can return.

When I came to Maine more than thirty years ago and bought the house I have lived in ever since (built in 1852, an old house by local standards), it was not the age of the house that impressed me but its location looking out to sea. I rescued the house from collapse, did what I could to restore its century-old character, and have enjoyed living in it. Then, quite suddenly a few years ago, I found it had grown to be the most comforting spot I know. When I have to leave it I can scarcely wait to return. My happiness begins when, bound east, I cross the Maine border at Kittery; and it increases slowly as the miles are laid behind me, until my car crests that long hill coming into Lincolnville, where the whole broad expanse of Penobscot Bay opens up before me. From there my joy builds at every turn of the road—until my first sight of Blue Hill, with its white houses and pointed steeples nestling in the trees at the head of the bay, tells me I shall soon be home. As I press on, each mile of the road becomes more familiar. Finally I recognize each separate house and I know who lives in most of them; I know the flowers in the gardens and the trees towering over the roofs. There is one house with red phlox in the dooryard; I do not envy that man his wife, nor his ox, nor his ass, nor anything that is his except that phlox.

When I reach my own village and pass the little red grade school with children playing in front of it; when I see the church, the cemetery, the library, and the store, and turn onto the Naskeag Point road, a feeling of affection wells up within me that no other place on all this green earth could duplicate. I am indeed at home.

I suppose there are many villages like this in Maine and many more in America, but no other place would provide for me the same feeling of comfort and protection. It is as though I were encompassed about by strong walls where no evil could befall me, and where all things and occurrences are familiar and manageable. Everyone's life is an amalgam of fact and dream. We all live our lives within some sort of protective shells of our own contrivance that shield us from the blasts of the outside world. Life would not be possible if we were not able to temper the harsh realities we face with life as we would have it. We all need, somewhere, the "most comforting spot in all America."

The Bar Harbor Express

ON RARE OCCASIONS it gets uncomfortably hot in Maine, but never for long. It was up to eighty-four degrees at Amen Farm recently and nearly ninety in Ellsworth, temperatures that in other parts of the country would be nothing to get excited about, but here they have everybody with their collars open, behaving as though they were going to collapse of a heat stroke. I felt that way myself, but when I came downstairs this morning and opened the door to the breezes off the bay, the temperature was back to a reasonable fifty-eight degrees.

It is a good thing we do get a few hot days once in a while, just to make us appreciate how fortunate we usually are. I worked in Philadelphia for many years, where temperatures above ninety degrees—with corresponding humidity—are commonplace. I can remember having to don a freshly laundered seersucker suit every morning before going to my office in order to look presentable. This was, of course, in the days before man-made fabrics. There was no air-conditioning either, and people got pretty uncomfortable by late afternoon. On really bad days, I would check on the state of affairs about four o'clock by walking around the office and seeing how many of the stenographers had dark patches on the back of their dresses. If there were many, I would close the office and send them home early. I don't know that they were any more comfortable elsewhere, but at least they had a change of location in which to perspire.

I can easily understand why, in the days before air-conditioning (which is not so long ago) families who could afford to spent the summer in Maine. In my Philadelphia days there was not such a wholesale removal as there had been prior to, let us say, 1930, but the big Maine summer "cottages" were still used. To accommodate the summer people, trains like the Bar Harbor Express and the Gull and others often ran in several sections. The Bar Harbor, probably the most famous of the trains, originated in Washington, D.C., and increased in length as it progressed to the north and east. Additions were made to the train in Baltimore and Philadelphia, and by the time it pulled out of the Pennsylvania Station in New York there might be several day coaches, eight or more sleepers, two diners, and a couple of club cars. From Portland on, the train was broken up as parts of it were detoured to Rangeley, Rockland, and Ellsworth.

In my early days as a Bar Harbor Express traveler I summered near Camden, so I rode in the Rockland section. I was usually awakened by the train being taken apart in Brunswick, but all I did was raise the blind a little to verify my location and then go back to sleep until the Pullman porter called me at Damariscotta. The train was hardly an express on these local stretches of track, so I still had plenty of time to dress and wander into the club car, where the waiter/cook would stir up some scrambled eggs and bacon for me.

One of the many pleasant aspects about traveling on the Bar Harbor was that the train crews seldom varied and that every week you saw the same passengers, most of whom you knew casually at least. I know from experience that the conductor always kept a few spare berths or roomettes for emergencies. I recall one occasion (undoubtedly there were others) when I had forgotten to make a reservation and had caught the train at the last minute, expecting to have to sit up in a day coach. But the conductor, who knew me, smiled and said, "Don't worry. Just sit in the club car and cool off for a few minutes until we get going, and I'll fix you up." He did, and if you are wondering why he said for me to sit and cool off, it was because in pre–air-conditioned days large blocks of ice were loaded into mysterious compartments under the cars, whence cooled air was blown into the passenger accommodations.

It is not just the nostalgia of the elderly that makes me think travel was more comfortable and dignified in days gone by. What comparison can there be between lugging your baggage around for miles in big, overcrowded airports (to ride finally in an equally overcrowded airplane) and having a polite and efficient Redcap (and they were polite and efficient in those days) take your bags so you would not have to worry about them any more. The bags would be in your car when you got there. The Pullman porter in his spotless white jacket would usher you to your seat or compartment in a spacious car, dust off your hat and put it in a paper bag on the rack over your head, ask if he could get you a drink, and probably offer you a newspaper.

The world may have improved in some ways, though I am not quite sure what they are except for medicine, but it most certainly has gone backward where public transportation is concerned.

Summer

Cottage Gardens

I SUPPOSE MORE people of moderate means have traveled to Europe and England in the last twenty years than in all the previous years of this century. The airplane, of course, made this possible. People did not go abroad in masses before, not so much because of the cost, but on account of the time involved. Passage by water consumed five or six days each way, which left precious little time out of a two-week vacation for sightseeing. I have been made aware of this change by the number of people visiting my garden who recognize it as a reasonable facsimile of a small English garden.

Obviously, many visitors to England do not go with the idea of devoting much time to gardens—and if they do plan to see any, they are gardens connected with "stately homes." However, if travelers can get out of London and escape their tour guide long enough, they cannot fail to observe that almost every house is surrounded by a garden. These are the gardens mine reminds them of, and are what they think they would like to see around their own homes. Cottage gardens, which mine vaguely resembles, have perennial appeal because they are compact, colorful, and appear to need little continued attention once planted. This latter is not quite true, as I can attest, but cottage gardens are colorful and usually manageable. One thinks of them as brimming with old-fashioned flowers and fragrant shrubs; with clematis climbing the walls, roses looping the fences, and hollyhocks and delphiniums swinging in the breeze.

The English, who were great travelers during the days of the Empire, carried the idea of a cottage garden along with them wherever they happened to be stationed, even though climatic conditions often made one impossible. But they tried anyway, and the ideal they sought became a recognizable art form. Helen Allingham, a nineteenth-century English watercolorist, made the cottage garden her special field. She painted hundreds of pictures of them, which, though differing in detail, are archetypical. I have one hanging on the wall of my study, called *In a Surrey Garden*, and on my bookshelves I have several books filled with color reproductions of others. Mrs. Allingham painted cottages and people in and around them, too. A delicate "Olde Worlde" flavor permeates all of her watercolors. I mention this characteristic because if one wants a cottage garden, her paintings point the way.

The very earliest gardens in England were of course utilitarian. A Tudor statute of 1589 ruled that no cottages were to be constructed unless four acres of land were set aside for the use of the inhabitants. (This idea, limited of course to people living in the country, was brought by the Pilgrims to America and is one of the reasons the houses were set well apart in our old New England villages, though they did not all have four acres of land.) While gardens as large as four acres were meant to afford space for fruit, vegetables, and animals, it cannot have been long before flowers were included. By Helen Allingham's time there seem to have been more flowers that vegetables, although even today some vegetables rub shoulders with flowers in most English cottage gardens. In my own garden, although I have a separate kitchen garden, garlic, parsley, chives, rosemary, and other herbs share space with the flowers.

In making a cottage garden there is one inviolable rule, and that is that the garden must be casual. There should not be too much grass, and the closest the garden may come to formality is in the use of edging plants. It must not be sophisticated and run to color schemes and allées. The essence of an "Allingham" garden was in its tumble of whatever the gardener liked—usually something he was given—all being planted together, with the only planning being to keep the tall plants toward the back.

The prettiest small English cottage garden I have ever seen was owned by Margery Fish, who lived in the Somerset village of East Lambrook Manor. I mention the place specifically because some reader may be in the area, and the garden is well worth visiting. It is an outstanding example of how much can be grown, and grown well, in a small space. It is filled to overflowing with great masses of old-fashioned flowers and shrubs. Mrs. Fish, who died a few years ago, wrote a number of garden books, one of which, *Cottage Garden Flowers*, was published in this country by Transatlantic Arts, Inc., Hollywood-by-the-Sea, Florida. This book is well worth the attention of those who cannot visit East Lambrook Manor.

Memories

AMONG THE THOUSAND or so books on gardening I am lucky enough to own, is one called *The Tranquil Gardener*, written by Robert Gaythorne-Hardy, a well-known English gardener and writer. He said that when he had assembled the book—from pieces he had written for several magazines and newspapers—he cast about for a title and thought, since the book was a job of assembly rather than a new creation, he would call it "The Lazy Gardener." It developed, though, that this title had been preempted by some other lazy gardener, so he settled for "The Tranquil Gardener," thinking as I do, I suppose, that tranquility is the most important feature of a garden.

I doubt Mr. Gaythorne-Hardy's book had a very large sale in this country. I bought my copy at Henry Sotheran's bookshop on Sackville Street in London a few years ago, when I was wandering along looking in the store windows lining that delightful old thoroughfare. I say I doubt it had a large sale in America, because there is nothing it it that instructs one on how to grow things. In this respect it is similar to many other English garden books. What they do is to create an interest and a desire to know more, and perhaps to possess such a garden, but if you want to know how to be a gardener you have to go elsewhere for your instruction. Americans, on the other hand, being a busy, bustling people ever mindful of having the first peas or growing the largest cabbage or marigold on the block, want to be told how to do it. They are not interested in hearing from Mr. Gaythorne-Hardy, or anyone else, the following:

> I had always been told how my father, as a young man sixty years ago and more, had found the Leucojum on the Thames not far from Oxford, where he was an undergraduate. About a year ago I went with loving piety to the place; after some searching by boat I came to a backwater and there, around the banks, they resplendently were.

It is possible you may not even recognize a Leucojum by that name, as it is better known among gardeners unfamiliar with botanical nomenclature as a Spring Snowflake (*Leucojum vernum*) or a Summer

Snowflake (*Leucojum aestivum*). Both kinds look like giant snowdrops and should be in everyone's garden. They do best in a sheltered position and prefer a sandy or gravelly soil. But there, you see, my American blood shows up—I am telling you how to grow them.

It is of course a very good thing to know how to grow plants, and the bookshops are filled with expensive paperbacks—and even more expensive hardcover books—that will provide in the greatest detail all the information you could ask for. Jim Crockett's *Victory Garden* is a fine example. If you own that book—and who does not?—and follow orders, you will be able to grow everything he writes about just as well as he says you will. But I am not sure this is what gardening is all about.

The title of Mr. Gaythorne-Hardy's book gives a clue. I am glad he did not use the "Lazy Gardener" title, because "The Tranquil Gardener" comes much closer to grasping the real purpose of a garden. Beds of flowers or rows of vegetables are attractive and profitable and I do not decry them, but they have little to do with a quiet and peaceful retreat that invites you to sit, putting aside for a while the pressures of the day, steeping yourself in tranquility. Of course you may not want tranquility, in which case I give you my blessing and speed you on your way, although I hope you occasionally take time to sit and ponder upon where it is you are going.

I have sat in quite a lot of different gardens around the world. My purpose was not to find the most beautiful rose or the most magnificent rhododendron, but rather just a breath of that almost magical aura that envelops one in a tranquil garden. In Japan it can be found in the austerity of a sea of sand, a stone lantern, and a twisted pine, with a wood block for a seat; in a Chinese garden where the overpowering presence is a large pitted rock; in an English cottage garden, all flowers and bees and thatch; or in a garden like that of the Spite House in Rockport, Maine, where with perennial borders on either hand, you glimpse the heaving ocean through wind-torn spruces.

One does not need perfection in a garden. That can be achieved (if you have money enough) by employing a battery of gardeners. In fact, some of the most appealing gardens I have known have been a little down at heel—but the presence was there. My own garden certainly does not have this aura everywhere, but there are spots where I can sit and feel time flow by me and around me, where I become a part of eternity and not just a chip hurled along on time's surface.

Summer

61

Gaythorne-Hardy spoke of his father's Leucojum. I don't have any descendants of the flowers in the garden where I grew up, but I have gifts from other gardens and gardeners that recall happy days of the past. Outside my greenhouse door are a pair of lavenders, now in full bloom, that came from the Berkshire hills; beside one of the many boulders with which God blessed my garden are several pasqueflowers, grown from seed plucked from a plant in an old friend's garden in Hampshire—he is now long gone to celestial gardens where weeds never grow, but they remind me of him; growing in odd chinks and crannies are plants of Kenilworth ivy I pulled from an ancient wall surrounding the school I attended as a boy; and there is a copper beech twenty feet tall that young friends brought me from Pennsylvania that many years ago.

A garden is a place where the flowers of memory grow strong and sweet, and time for a while stands still.

Choice

AT A COCKTAIL PARTY one night, a lady cornered me and complained that I had been writing too many gloomy articles, "all about dying and the like," and that I should stop it. I pled innocence, but as she took no notice of my disclaimer and carried on with her theme, I decided to look things over when I got home to see if there was any merit to her complaint. I could find none. It is true that one February I wrote a review of a book called *The View from Eighty*, but neither my review nor the book itself seemed to me to be very gloomy. After all, when one is past eighty, just good sense makes one realize that time is running out, but that is no cause for gloom. Each new day is still all bright, brand-new, and sparkling, just as it was when you were eighteen, but your options as to how you will use the day are different.

Yes, in one of my columns I did quote Shakespeare's "A man can die but once, we owe God a death," and I acknowledge that the remembrance of that quotation was because my wife's mother, who had lived with us for a decade, had recently died. However, she was in her ninety-fifth year and well satisfied to depart life's problems, which become a bit troublesome at that age. While we shall miss her, the remembrance of her personality outweighs the sadness. She was of the old school. She had worked all her active life, and had the most withering contempt for people who did not have a job. "Unemployment!" she said, "I was never unemployed. There is always a job if you will take what is offered. Maybe you won't like it, but so what! Take it until you can get something better." Her other fetish was cleanliness. "Soap is cheap, and water is free," she announced early and often.

"Mom," as she was known, was a simple person and her wants were few. She read the *Bangor Daily News* and the Bible and watched Lawrence Welk on television. She was fiercely independent and had about the same respect for people who used credit cards as she did for those who failed to bathe. If she did not have the money for something, she didn't buy it. The thing that must make her most happy in the hereafter is the knowledge that after her death we found a couple of small insurance policies that, together with her Social Security death benefit, were enough to pay her funeral expenses. Paying her own way to the last.

But there, I have been writing about death again, although I don't think it gloomy. Anyway, the lady who scolded me should know that essayists don't choose their subjects; the subjects choose them. Political and sportswriters, for instance, have no freedom at all—they just write about politics and sports. Even a freewheeling writer like this one, with no special subject, has one determined for him. I don't get up some morning and decide to write about eels, as I did a few weeks ago; it happened because eels swam across my radar screen. I saw some in a dish in the fish-shop and bought one for our supper, then I got home and saw the eel-spear in our dining room, and that further motivated me. Before sitting down to my typewriter, however, I thought I had better do a little research, because my only previous knowledge of eels was based on some smoked ones I had eaten in Holland and a few I had caught up a creek that fed Megunticook Lake, not far from an island I once owned. I knew rather vaguely that eels breed in the Sargasso Sea, but everyone knows that. The result was that I spent a fascinating couple of hours boning up on eels, both alive and in the pan. This suggests to you, I hope, that I get as much fun (or more) out of these essays as you do. I hope it proves also, or indicates anyway, that when I write "gloomy" pieces, it is not because I am gloomy—I seldom am—but because some event has suggested a subject.

Philosophers have been arguing about free will for thousands of years. I am still on the fence. I agree that I have the freedom to choose; did not the famous Doctor Johnson say, "Sir, we know our will is free, and there's an end on't"? It was a way the good doctor had of ending any argument when he was not sure he was going to win it, but it is not very convincing. I like better the historian Froude's remark that "to deny the freedom of the will is to make morality impossible." But man is a frail and lonely barque on the vast ocean of life and—like the Portuguese man-of-war—is moved by every wind that blows. Almost everything we do is influenced by something that has gone before; my choice of material for this essay is no exception.

Mealtimes

A FRIEND ASKED me the other day if I knew anything about mealtimes in the eighteenth century. I replied that I did, but later, when I came to write down what I knew, found I needed to check my sources. As my friend remarked, people don't make notes or diary entries of things that are commonplace, things they do every day, things that everybody knows. Of course, everybody knows about them at the time, but everybody does not know about them two hundred years later.

If you look back far enough you can be pretty sure that before men herded animals or cultivated gardens, they ate, like other animals, whenever there was something to eat. They had no regular mealtimes. Graminivorous animals eat all the time; if you have ever lived with sheep or cattle, you know that when they are in a pasture they eat constantly. If your cows are lying down, the chances are they are chewing their cud; otherwise they drift across a field, grazing as they go. Sheep feed the same way, in the middle of the night too, if they are not sleeping—and from my observation they sleep only in short naps. Deer do the same thing. They graze my hayfield just like cattle, and if the field is snow-covered they invade my garden and eat practically everything except the rosebushes. They are as destructive as oversized goats in their feeding habits and will eat almost anything, including the tips of azaleas, arborvitaes, junipers, or grass—whatever is vegetable in character.

In spite of the vegetarian cult's defection from meat, the truth is that mankind started out, and remains, omnivorous. We still have the remains of some tearing teeth in our mouths. At the dawn of the race we stuffed ourselves, like all other animals, when the tribe was lucky enough to kill a large game animal—and made do with berries, seeds, roots, mice, and toads when times were tough. Civilization took a giant leap forward when men learned how to imprison animals so they could be slaughtered when food was needed. Later, when we learned to sow and harvest crops also, we began to eat at regular times. I don't know what those times were, but I would guess there was a morning meal, because your stomach is empty when you get up, and an evening meal, because you are hungry after being awake all day. We haven't changed a great deal except that as subsistence (for some of us) came more easily, we slipped in a few extra meals. We still celebrate special occasions by stuffing ourselves, just as did our prehistoric ancestors.

But to get back to the eighteenth century: we don't know too much about when the workers ate, as they didn't keep records—and the people who were better off didn't keep records for them. For the blue-collar folks (though that term hadn't yet been coined), a lot of work was done before breakfast—and still is on farms, where the milking and other chores are taken care of before the men sit down to the first real meal of the day.

In the 1700s the middle-class folk and the gentry didn't usually get to breakfast until about ten o'clock, and all they had then was coffee or tea, and rolls or bread and butter. In the previous century, Pepys made a point of stopping somewhere for a "dram" on the way to his office (beer usually, but sometimes wine or something more authoritative), and most others seemed to do the same thing. They met and discussed business over "break-fast." The important meal was dinner, which came in the middle of the day. Author and diarist Fanny Burney says, in 1768, "We breakfast always at 10 . . . we dine precisely at 2 . . . drink tea about 6 . . . and sup exactly at 9." Of course Fanny was in pretty high society, and it is reasonable to suppose that working people's mealtimes were dictated, as they still are, by the necessities of their employment.

In 1741 William Byrd of Westover, Virginia, whose job was keeping an eye on his slaves and occasionally going to Williamsburg to attend sessions in the courthouse, writes "[I] rose about 5, read Hebrew and Greek. I prayed and had tea . . . I played the fool with Sally, God forgive me. I wrote letters till dinner and ate roast beef." On another day, "[I] rose about 5 . . . I prayed and had tea with Col. Grimes . . . About 9 went to council, then to court where we sat until 2, and then dined with Wetherburn." I don't know who Sally was, and I don't have time to read the diary again to find out, but I judge she was one of his slaves. He also "played the fool" with Marjorie, and somebody he identified as "F-r-b-y," and as usual asked God to forgive him. (I guess He did.) Byrd never mentions supper, so dinner must have been the one substantial meal of the day.

Mealtimes are largely a geo-socio-economic matter. Here in Maine, and I would judge in most of this part of the country, those who work with their hands and get on the job by seven a.m. eat their breakfast about six, their midday meal—called "dinner"—at about eleven, and supper at about five or half-past five in the afternoon. Normally they also have a snack of some sort before retiring. The white-collar set, and those of us with urban disciplines, break our fast about seven or eight a.m., have a midday meal we call lunch around noon, and sit down to dinner anywhere from six to eight in the evening. I have found it interesting that among working people the word "luncheon" is seldom used but "lunch" is—although it does not necessarily mean a midday meal but rather signifies something to eat at any time.

When you eat your meals depends not only on your employment, but also on where in the world you are. In Spanish-speaking countries breakfast is around eight a.m., but luncheon is not served until after two p.m., and continues until about four. Obviously on that schedule you cannot dine when we do, so dinner doesn't start until about nine in the evening. If you were to go into a restaurant in Spain or Latin America looking for dinner at six in the evening, the waiters would still be clearing up the dishes after luncheon.

The further I get into this subject, the more interesting it becomes—and the more impossible it seems to be to cover it briefly—so

I hand the subject to you, with my blessing. Perhaps you can ponder upon it instead of counting sheep the next time you suffer from insomnia.

Thoreau

I DO NOT KNOW how long it is since I first read *Walden*, but it must be fifty-five years at least. I have always found something in Thoreau to appeal to me, because he was a countryman-philosopher, which, in a humble way, I consider myself to be. Even so, I could never warm to his poetry; it always seemed so angular and bristling. On the other hand, when one reads his prose, one feels the undertow of a mighty swell that could be nothing *less* than poetry.

I say I could not warm to his poetry. I mean his formal verse, which I stumble over, although in *Walden* there is one piece included in the chapter "House-Warming" that I liked so well I had part of it painted on the heavy lintel over my study fireplace in a house where I once lived:

LIGHT-WINGED SMOKE, ICARIAN BIRD,

MELTING THY PINIONS IN THY UPWARD FLIGHT,

. . . GO THOU MY INCENSE UPWARD FROM THIS HEARTH,

AND ASK THE GODS TO PARDON THIS CLEAR FLAME.

I never see smoke spiraling from the chimney of a Maine cottage on a wintry day, without "Light-winged Smoke, Icarian bird" coming to my tongue.

I said there was a ground swell of poetry in Thoreau's prose, and I have had my feeling confirmed by Dr. William M. White, professor of English at Virginia Polytechnic Institute and State University. His book *All Nature Is My Bride* (published by the Chatham Press of Old Greenwich, Connecticut, 1975) consists of passages from Thoreau's journals arranged as poetry.

I have a bad habit of buying books as they are published and then not reading them until much later. I think this better, however, than finding a book you think you would be interested in and then deferring its purchase until it may be out of print—or you forget about it. I bought *All Nature Is My Bride* some years ago, but got around to reading it only after a long time-lapse. However, I have read it twice recently, and will keep it for a bedside book, as it should be enjoyed in small sips like a fine wine. Knowing something about books, I can appreciate the work and talent that went into the gathering and arranging of an anthology like this.

The extracts stretch from 1837 to 1861. While one is conscious of maturing thought as the years pass, it is obvious that Thoreau came into this world *sui generis*, and the essence of his genius is as apparent in his youth, when he was but twenty, as it is when he died at forty-four. Ralph Waldo Emerson best expressed Thoreau's value to the world, when he ended his eulogy with these words:

> . . . *He had in a short life exhausted the capabilities of this world; wherever there is knowledge; wherever there is virtue; wherever there is beauty, he will find a home.*

I am grateful to Professor White for solving the mystery of Thoreau's poetry for me, but equally for pointing me to new magic in his prose. Thoreau has messages for everybody. When I was young I could read

> WHAT SHALL I DO WITH THIS HOUR,
>
> SO LIKE TIME
>
> AND YET SO FIT FOR ETERNITY

and spill hours through my fingers, oblivious to their passing. But now I am old I can understand

> YELLOW GREEN WITH SPRING,
>
> YELLOW AND RIPE WITH AUTUMN
>
> . . . DRINK OF EACH SEASON'S INFLUENCE AS A VIAL,
>
> A TRUE PANACEA OF ALL REMEDIES
>
> MIXED FOR YOUR SPECIAL USE.

A Countryman's Farewell

68

Because I live looking out to sea, with fields and woods around me and never a dwelling in sight but the lighthouse on Green Island, I still live with nature—although I no longer walk as far as Thoreau walked. I have to go but a hundred paces and the spruces are around me, their needles under foot. The lichens on the rocks by my dooryard are as colorful as flowers:

> THE LICHENS REMEMBER THE SEA TODAY.
> THE USUALLY DRY CLADONIAS,
> WHICH ARE CRISP UNDER THE FEET,
> ARE FULL OF MOIST VIGOR.
> THE ROCKS SPEAK AND TELL THE TALES
> INSCRIBED ON THEM.
> THEIR INSCRIPTIONS ARE BROUGHT OUT,
> I PAUSE TO STUDY THEIR GEOGRAPHY.

In Thoreau's last journal entry, he wrote

> ALL THIS IS PERFECTLY DISTINCT TO AN OBSERVANT EYE,
> AND YET COULD EASILY PASS UNNOTICED BY MOST.
> THUS EACH WIND IS SELF-REGISTERING.

If you like Thoreau, do buy this book and keep it on your bedside table. (If you are a stranger to him, or if you think you cannot be his friend, buy it anyway.) He does not shine in a new light, but in a clearer one.

Woodbines

A FELLOW ESSAYIST in the *Berkshire Eagle*, Richard Nunley, wrote a piece a few years ago about the climbing plant we call woodbine. As he said, it is also known as the Virginia creeper, and is botanically *Parthenocissus quinquefolia*. I have one tumbling over a stone wall separating my land from the highway, and very colorful it is in the autumn. However, the part of Mr. Nunley's story that interested me most was his reference to Woodbine cigarettes.

When I was a boy growing up in England, cigarettes had a class structure just like the rest of society in that class-conscious country. In the upper reaches of cigarette nobility were a few brands such as De Reske or Benson and Hedges. There was also a Russian cigarette, the name of which I can no longer recall, which was about twice as long as the others. About a third of its length was a pasteboard tube, which sophisticates pinched in both directions between thumb and forefinger, making a crude filter cigarette—although I assure you the pinching was just affectation, and not done with any thought that it helped prevent lung cancer. Perhaps medical people knew about lung cancer then, but no one else gave it a thought, and if people died of it, it was a well-kept secret.

Socially, the middle-class cigarettes were Goldflakes and Players —I think both brands survive to this day—but the cigarettes of the masses, definitely lower-class, were Woodbines. They were a bit thinner than other cigarettes and came five to the pack, in a fragile green paper sheaf that offered a minimum of protection. The price was a penny— that is to say an English penny, known colloquially as a copper. It was worth at that time two American cents, because the pound sterling stood at $4.80 and there were 240 pennies to the pound.

I doubt that Woodbines were made of the finest tobacco (though it was supposed to be Virginia leaf), but as I recall them through the haze of years and smoke, they did not taste much worse than other cigarettes. The lower classes (whom the CIO and AFL now call "workers," as though no one else worked) had a lot of unkind things to say about Woodbines. People suggested, for example, that Woodbines were filled with dried horse manure—which in those days blew around the streets in clouds any time rain had not fallen for a couple of days— but they smoked them because Woodbines were cheap. Come to think of it, no cigarette really tastes *good*, so you might as well learn to like the cheapest. (I feel the same way about whiskey.) I still have recollections of crouching in the shelter of whatever was handy, in the omnipresent rain of the First World War, trying to light a Woodbine before it got so wet that the feat was impossible. In those far-off days book-matches had not yet been invented, and the best bet was a wax vesta. These were quite a bit shorter than the modern match and were apt to burn your fingers, but because they were made of twisted cotton impregnated with wax, they would burn, briefly, even in a deluge.

I think Woodbines won the first World War for the British, although, as in World War II, it was a Pyrrhic victory. I have seen badly wounded men whose only concern was for a fag. (A fag in those days meant a cigarette, not a homosexual.) Somehow or other someone always had a Woodbine that could be lighted to push between the lips of a soldier so bandaged that all that could be seen was his mouth. When the hospital trains reached the channel ports, there were girls waiting with more Woodbines, and in all the little kits given by the Red Cross, Woodbines were included.

I smoked heavily all during my youth, but gave up the habit forty-five years ago, long before cigarettes were thought to endanger one's health. My reason for stopping was because after burning up about three packs a day, I usually found myself with a paralyzing headache at quitting time. One day I took myself in hand, opened my office window (overlooking Walnut Street in Philadelphia), and after emptying all the cigarettes I could find into a file-box, cast them into the outer darkness and never smoked again. I have often thought the "going home" crowd on Walnut Street that day must have been mystified by the rain of Chesterfields.

Here in the States, Sweet Caporals and Bull Durhams fell into the Woodbine class. (I have not seen either for years.) With Bull Durhams you had to roll your own, as the tobacco came in a little cotton bag with a drawstring. You shook the tobacco onto the flimsy cigarette paper, held it in one hand while you used your other hand and your teeth to close the bag, and then rolled your cigarette. Of course if you were a cowhand, railroad worker, or other hard-case type, you did your rolling one-handed. I never achieved that dizzy eminence; I had trouble enough doing it with both hands—and, at that, usually lost about half the tobacco.

What a wealth of memories the name Woodbine recalls. Thank you, Mr. Nunley.

Summer Chapel

Y ESTERDAY WAS ONE of those perfect Maine days we exclaim
about so enthusiastically that foreigners believe our weather is like that
all the time. Unfortunately it is not—or perhaps fortunately, because
if it were, we would not appreciate it enough when we do have it.
When I got up about six o'clock this morning there was a little offshore
fog, but it soon dissipated with the strengthening sun. The day developed clear, cool, and sunny, with scarcely a cloud. It was just the sort
of day that Mrs. Todd described—"But I don't know's we shall have a
better day all the rest of the summer"—when she was thinking of an
expedition to Green Island. (I speak, of course, of the immortal Mrs.
Almira Todd, of Sarah Orne Jewett's *Country of the Pointed Firs*.)

We were not planning an expedition to Green Island, although
there *is* a Green Island lying a couple of miles offshore in front of
Amen Farm. No, what we planned was an expedition to another of
Maine's long peninsulas, forty-odd miles down the coast, to hear an old
minister for whom we have a great affection. We arrived early and
pulled off the road onto the grass, leaving tire-tracks in the dew that
still sparkled in the sunshine. There were a few others there before us,
mostly ancient citizens like ourselves who need a little extra time to
get out of cars and navigate the steps into church and pew. The young
ones came later, but there were plenty of them when they did arrive,
refuting a commonly held idea (by those who know no better) that
churches—all, that is, but those of the self-proclaimed moral majority
—have been deserted by the upcoming generation. Churches are not
dying on the vine in Maine, and I doubt they are elsewhere. We have
few padlocked churches, and the only ones that are not in current use
are those built in horse-and-buggy days, before one could jump into a
car and in twenty minutes drive to a large church serving a wider community. Regional churches now gather more communicants under
their wings, just as regional high schools gather students. The small,
lonely churches you sometimes see boarded up on back roads are redun-
dant, like the little red schoolhouses near them.

But I digress. The church we were visiting was one of the many
nondenominational chapels built around the turn of the century by

local summer communities, composed of people whose cottages on the peninsulas were far from the villages and local churches. A few of these houses of worship (usually where Episcopalians predominated) were built of stone, in imitation of the little country churches in England, but most were constructed of frame and shingle. For me they are delightful: uniformly small, unobtrusive, retiring little chapels, often with just a touch of "carpenter's Gothic" about them. Those of us not bereft of our sense of smell recognize immediately the odor of shingles and sawed wood that lingers around them long years after the workmen who built them packed their tools and eventually went to join their ancestors in the village graveyards. Another distinguishing feature of these small houses of God is that they have no graveyards. They are open for worship only from about the Fourth of July until Labor Day, for that is as long as their parishioners are around. They have no resident ministers, but as almost all summer colonies number a few retired or vacationing members of the cloth, they are well-served.

People settled themselves comfortably (as comfortably as anyone can in a church pew), the harmonium and a couple of members playing recorders tuned up, and the service got started. The chapel was fuller than usual, because in addition to the regular service there were to be a christening and a wedding. The christening was exactly as christenings should be. The parents (who had been married by that minister a couple of years before) mounted the dais, and the baby, who didn't like any part of it, began to yell. He continued to voice his disapproval until he was taken into the preacher's arms, when, overawed by his sudden elevation to the center of the stage, he fell silent. We didn't stay for the wedding—although anyone who wished to stay was invited—and after stopping at the door long enough to tell the preacher how much we enjoyed the sermon, we wandered out into the warm sunshine to join our friends and head off for Sunday brunch. While this may shock a few of my more orthodox readers, I shall have to confess that as a preamble to my food I imbibed a tall, cool bloody mary.

So much is said and written nowadays about the dominance of the more unpleasant side of life that I should like to raise my small voice in protest. Certainly there is evil in the world, and always will be, but the great majority of people are decent, family-loving, hardworking, ordinary citizens, whose only acquaintance with mortal sin is when they see it on television. Millions of Americans did as I did this morning. Perhaps they did not all attend church, but that is unimportant. What counts is what went on in their heads, and that for the most part was innocent—and probably thoughtful of their families and neighbors. I just hope that they had as beautiful a day as I did, and, if they felt like it, bloody marys before lunch.

AUTUMN

A haze on the far horizon
    The infinite, tender sky,
The ripe rich tint of the cornfields,
    And the wild geese flying high—
And all over upland and lowland
    The charm of the golden rod—
Some of us call it autumn
    And others call it God.
                    —From Each in His Own Tongue,
                        by William Herbert Carruth

75

Diaries

Having Kept A diary for most of my life, I frequently turn to it to learn what I was doing and thinking on the same date in previous years. It is an illuminating pursuit. I wish I had all the years of my life recorded, but in addition to the lacunae created occasionally by my tiring of the discipline of writing each day, many volumes have been mislaid or destroyed. One set I would especially like to have covered the last years of the First World War and up to 1923. They lie (what is left of them) on the bottom of the Pacific Ocean, halfway between Honolulu and Los Angeles. I abandoned them when I made a rapid departure (in only my pants and undershirt, carrying my sextant) from a ship called *City of Honolulu*, which caught fire and subsequently sank. However, those diaries I do have extend back back to 1943, and they reveal enough of what I was doing, and how I felt about things, to enable me to sketch in a fairly accurate picture of the latter years of my life.

I am not always pleased with what I read. We are apt to think of ourselves as being much wiser and better people than we really are, but an honest diary is an effective prescription for correcting one's misconceptions. The best diaries are a blend of self-revelation and recording. They tell what the diarist is doing and what he thinks about it and other people involved. Pepys and Kilvert are outstanding examples of good diarists. Harold Nicholson's is the finest diary of the twentieth century.

Thinking it might interest or amuse you, I will quote from my own diary entries (edited) for the same day from 1974 to 1978:

1974

Heavy fog. Telephoned Mexico to talk to Golding about a visit. He seems as indestructible as ever. He was just thrown from his horse and dragged thirty to forty feet before he could get his foot out of the stirrup.

Frank, who is going to be around a few days, took us to Eatons' to eat a lobster. He is a gourmet. He told me he paid $17,000 for his new car, a Mercedes, about twice what a Lincoln would cost and I think not as comfortable. He drove us to Eatons' and took all the corners on two wheels to demonstrate its cornering ability. I told him

Carters Point Road was full of pot-holes but he went over it at 50 mph anyway and damned near put us in the ditch. I love him in spite of it.

Telephone call from Craftsbury Common. They can't accommodate us on account of all the leaf-peepers.

To the young Richmonds' and ate clams and potato salad. Everybody got a mild sunburn except me. I got mine in the garden months ago. Late getting home but hurried off to the yacht club to a C'tail party. We were late arriving and early leaving. Home to find the deepfreeze kaput and the temperature up to 42 degrees.

1975

Labor Day, but almost no one labors nowadays. Picked ten pints of blueberries and finished a rough copy of my piece for Up Country.

1976

Home and found a message from —'s father. "She is still in critical condition — could go either way. Two broken legs, broken pelvis, broken vertebra, left hip blown to hell, lacerated liver, spline removed, large bowel cut, two-thirds lower jaw completely dismantled, right hand beat but not broken, etc., etc. She has strong will and is fighting like hell." Thus — verbatim. [She lived in spite of it all.] Got to bed and read about spiders until 10:30 p.m.

1977

Ellsworth all day. Hurried home, went to a cocktail party and met a lot of people we did not know. The hostess a dry, desiccated sort of woman — like artificial flowers — pleasant enough but gave me the feeling I belonged to a different race. Has summered in Maine all her life but knows not one of the native inhabitants. She might as well have been in British India during the days of the Raj. There are many around like her.

We dined at home. We were to have had sweetbreads but when Helen turned her back, the dogs stole them off the kitchen counter so we ate, instead, a can of beef stroganoff.

1978

Woke with a mild hangover but nothing that will convert me to abstinence. This has been a day of many interruptions. First, a charming young couple with two children stopped and wanted to speak to me.

They are readers of my column. They had been here before. They had read that I enjoyed wine so brought me a bottle. The woman, about thirty-five, one of the prettiest girls I have ever met. Her husband and children as charming. They took my picture. I could never escape the FBI. My photograph must be in every state of the union.

As a contrast, but just as pleasant, a cheerful lady of ninety-five, who has been a reader of my material for many years, escorted by her grand-nephew, called to see me in the flesh. She had once written me recommending I give my cow a pail of hot water, with thoroughwort in it, after the cow had calved. She was as lively and chirruping as a cricket. Her eyesight was a little impaired but otherwise she was as young as I.

We had one more caller: my friend Rocky, who stopped on his way home from the harbor and gave us a couple of cunners he had caught in his traps. I was grateful, for cunners make the best of all fish chowders.

These entries have been severely cut, but I hope they will convey a little of the pleasure there is to be gained from diary-keeping. Anyone can keep a diary. Arthur Ponsonby, M.P., an authority on diaries, says,

Diary writing is within the reach of every human being who can put pen to paper . . . people of all ages and degrees who have never ventured to write a line for publication . . . are able to keep a diary the value of which need not in any way suffer from their literary incapacity. On the contrary, literary talent may be a barrier to complete sincerity.

Try it, and you will find, if you have any curiosity about life and yourself, that keeping a diary is habit-forming.

Michaelmas

THE WIND, WHAT there is of it, is in the east. The clouds are close overhead, just hanging there, and a gentle rain is falling. The thermometer reads fifty degrees, but it feels colder. Not really cold enough to have a fire in my study grate, but I am going to light one anyway just for cheerfulness. Perhaps the wind is stronger than I think, as I can see the Michaelmas daisies, which have grown quite tall in the rich soil of my dooryard border, swaying from side to side in the little gusts.

Michaelmas, you know, is properly a church festival celebrated on September 29. Michael was—maybe still is—the archangel of the Jews. As I am not up on archangels, and not Jewish (nor a very good Christian either, I fear), the churchly observation of Michaelmas is not compelling upon me. What I remember of Michaelmas, as a child, is that it was traditionally the last day of the harvest, as Lammas Day was the first. I don't remember whether Michaelmas Sunday was the day when the altar steps were piled high with the harvest of the fields and gardens, or whether it was some other nearby date, but one way or another, Michaelmas was a colorful celebration. I think what it did for me was imprint me with the feeling that autumn is a happy time. I am left with a difficulty in understanding those who say they dread autumn, as it presages winter. Perhaps my view of the matter is like Scarlett O'Hara's would have been: autumn is a wonderful time, so why worry about winter? One reason I like autumn is because it does not spring upon us overnight as summer does—in Maine anyway.

A week ago I glimpsed the first distant color of fall while I was picking blueberries. I looked up and caught an azure flash as a blue jay scaled through the branches of a neighboring spruce. People talk about the harsh cry of the blue jay; it is harsh, but I think "metallic" comes a bit closer, just as its color may be distinguished as a metallic blue. Around here blue jays are resident all year, but I never see many except in autumn and winter. In the winter they crowd the bird-feeder and play second fiddle only to the crows and evening grosbeaks.

Another sign of the declining year is when, as I drive the country roads, doves, gravelling along the shoulders, fly up and then light ahead—just as the sanderlings do when I walk along the shore line. My old dog Quince, long gone to a doggy heaven (where I hope some day to join him), loved to chase sanderlings. They would allow him to get within a few feet, then rise in a flock and move on a little way up the beach, while he splashed through the water towards them. He made a couple of attempts at chasing doves, but I restrained him for fear he would forget where he was and run into a car.

A Countryman's Farewell

I think the Archangel Michael was fortunate in having our fall asters named after him. Those lovely autumn flowers we call Michaelmas daisies, now bowing and curtseying by my garden gate, are botanically *Aster novae angliae*, the New England aster. A dwarfed species, *A. novi-belgii*, about four feet tall (against the New England's six) are just as lovely in their own way, but do not have the variety or depth of color. Both spell fall, and take over when the late goldenrod fades. We had friends staying with us who had never been in Maine in the autumn, and they were overcome by the beauty of the asters. There is one stretch of a tenth of a mile on the road to the village where asters completely fill the roadside ditch with a lovely Quaker lavender.

In the autumn I travel with a spade in the back of my car, and when I see an aster of a color or type of growth I like, I stop and dig a part of it. (There is a wide color range from a delicate pink to a deep purple.) Asters transplant easily and you do no harm by taking part of a plant, for they are rank growers and will erase your larceny by the next year. Visitors to my garden admire them about as much as anything I grow and usually want to know where they can be bought. I tell them all they need is a spade and a sharp eye.

W. C. Bryant, in his poem "The Death of the Flowers," wrote: "The melancholy days are come, the saddest of the year, / Of wailing winds, and naked woods, and meadows brown and sere," but I like better the remark of the guide in the Katsura garden, in Kyoto: "When the flowers are gone, you can see the garden."

The Present Moment

WHEN A COLUMN I write received an award from the Maine Press Association as being the best of its class, I was pleased. I was pleased because it tickled my vanity, and I guess I have as much of that as the next man, but I was gratified also, because the fact the judges gave it an award supports a belief I have long held. Much has been written in recent years insisting the public taste is debased, and that the only things people are interested in are sex and violence. This I do not happen to believe; that the judges should choose my column for an award supports my belief, because if there is anything more remote from sex and violence than what I write, I have not read it. (Just in passing, I would like it to be understood that I am far from being opposed to sex. It is the greatest single mover in man's affairs, and most of it if fine and decent and the world could not survive without it. What I oppose is what passes for sex in the movies, on television, and in many modern novels.)

My mail, which is considerable, suggests that most people's lives are rather simple and relatively blameless. They have no objection to a tumble in the hay with a handsome lad or lassie, as the case may be, but they are not sex maniacs, nor do they spend too much time thinking about it. They live quiet, decent, useful lives—going to the supermarket, looking after their kids (or those of others), perhaps going to church, trying to balance checkbooks that usually seem to come out on the wrong side, and, in general, behaving themselves and facing life with their chins up.

I have always held that the way to a happy life is by keeping busy. This is particularly true as one ages, because the compulsions of daily affairs leave the young and middle-aged little time for pondering, while age and retirement—voluntary or compulsory—find one stripped of those demands, and if something is not done to fill the gap, loneliness and boredom move in.

Most of all, at any age, happy people are those who have learned to enjoy simple things. These are the people who write to me—perhaps this is why they read my newspaper column. I lay no claim to very profound erudition about any one thing, although I know a little about a lot of things. I know nothing of the burning questions of the day beyond what I read in the newspapers, and my column carefully avoids any suggestion that I do. What I do know something about is living, and what it takes to achieve what America's founding fathers said we should have—namely, the right to the pursuit of happiness, although they did not guarantee we would capture that elusive prize, described by Nathaniel Hawthorne as a butterfly, "which, when pursued, is always just beyond our grasp, but which, if you will sit down quietly, may alight upon you."

I heard a young woman on television this morning say that it would be a lovely day, that the sky would be blue with just a few mashed-potato clouds floating across it. Her metaphor made me chuckle; it was so apt but so absurd. All day long it has given me a quiet smile every time I have seen a cloud. Such small grains of manna lie around us constantly, waiting to be picked up, but we must enjoy them immediately because Holy Writ tell us we can't store manna for the next day. There is, after all, not really any tomorrow, any more than there is a yesterday. The only moment of sure life for me is the one that is here now as I press the keys of my typewriter.

I have a friend who is, by all our standards, very ill. She has inoperable cancer, which will probably be the cause of her death—though who knows? The point I would make is that she is not *dying of* cancer, but *living with* cancer. She is under no illusions about the state of her health, but although not comfortable physically, she is not wasting any of the precious time she has left. Her perceptions of the world we share have been heightened by her condition (as have mine because I am old), so she is living a month in every day, which is what we all should do. She says to me, every time we drive by one particularly lovely spot, where a little red boathouse overlooks a tiny harbor and small boats dance on miniature waves in the sparkling sunlight, "What a beautiful place we live in." And I echo, "Beautiful, indeed."

After church this morning, as I stood talking, something hurtled into me and grabbed my legs. When I looked down it was onto the flaxen head of a fellow parishioner, about a year old, who had just learned that the way to stay upright was—as in riding a bicycle—to keep moving, although she had not yet gotten the steering down pat. I thought how many days of sun and rain and happiness, and grief and love and content, would pass over those white-gold curls before she was my age. When I lifted her and looked into her young eyes that were all unafraid, I thought of my older friend, who had, just then, all that that little girl and all of us have—the present moment.

Doing Small Things Well

NANCY REMINDED ME of an appropriate little *bon mot* the other day: "Age is a question of mind over matter; if you don't mind it, it doesn't matter." It's a conclusion I had arrived at independently a long time ago. I am fairly well stricken in years, numerically, but I see dozens of people young enough to be my children acting as though they were candidates for admission to geriatric institutions. It has been my observation that they are the ones who have no compelling interest in their lives, and consequently devote most of their time to thinking about themselves. These are the people who have worked at some occupation, faithfully but with little inspiration, and let it go at that. They have come home from work and watched television or football, or played bridge or golf, and when they retired just threw away the free years that lay before them. All they aspired to was doing the same things, only more so.

Work should preeminently be the means of making a living. If your work is also a consuming passion, you are among the lucky ones. Most of us are not so fortunate, and labor, of necessity, at jobs that we do well enough but are not inspired by. The man who works all his life at something he thoroughly enjoys has no trouble with age and retirement, for he never grows old and he never retires. For the rest of us, the secret to happiness lies in having a second life outside of our employment. I don't mean just time-wasters like the things I mentioned in the preceding paragraph, but something we cannot wait to get to and, in many cases, make our mark at.

When the mail arrived yesterday it included among the flood of catalogues a slim package from Hatchards, a London bookseller. It was a book I had ordered nearly a year ago, entitled *The English Country Parson*. Hatchards had replied when I ordered it that the book was not yet published, but that they would send it as soon as it was. (I mention this to dispel any idea they are tardy in their attention to orders—they are not. I get books from them in many instances faster than I would from New York or Chicago.) Anyway, I was glad to have it, and mention it now because it contains a statement of Coventry Patmore's about a parson named William Barnes, who lived from 1801 to 1886. Patmore said, "He has done a small thing well, while his contemporaries have mostly been engaged in doing big things ill." Doing small things well is what we should be engaged in outside our employment, if our job is not providing us with a consuming interest. On the jacket blurb of *The English Country Parson* it is mentioned that one parson became a world authority on spiders, another was a famous rosarian, another a breeder of horses, and still another bred green mice. I am not suggesting we all raise green mice, but what I do recommend is that we emulate the Reverend William Barnes and do a small thing well.

The Maine magazine *Down East* has a section called "Making It in Maine." In one issue it told of three people who turned their interests into full-time jobs: one was a horologist, another a marine decorator, and a third made birchbark boxes decorated with porcupine quills. Every month the magazine lists additional examples— cabinetmakers, cake-bakers, old-tool collectors, you name it. Most of the people featured have turned their interests into paying occupations. That is fine if you choose to do so, but it is not necessary to make a business out of a hobby. (I don't like the word "hobby," as it connotes something unimportant, whereas what I am thinking of can be the biggest thing in your life.) What is important is that whatever it is, your chosen activity provides a centrality of interest that your employment failed to do.

We all change as we get older, which means we need, even more than we did while we were young, a consuming interest we can turn to. An elderly lady of my acquaintance said the other day that her habits had changed, and that things she thought would be eternal were proving transitory. She used to love letter-writing, but rarely nowadays puts pen to paper, and has no wish to. Babies, which she once adored, she is now happy to view from a distance. She no longer arranges flowers (which had been a great interest), and if she never went to another party, she acknowledged, that would be too soon. Now, you may say the great interest I recommend will fade too, and maybe it will, but it is less likely to, because even though a small thing, it is always presenting itself in new colors. Babies and bridge and correspondence and cocktails don't expand much. When you have learned what there is to know about them, there is nothing more. But of course, as Nancy said, "if you don't mind it, it doesn't matter."

North or South of the Tracks

WHEN VISITORS FROM more sophisticated parts visit us in summer or autumn (they never come in winter) they say how beautiful it is, but express dismay at the rich and the poor living cheek by jowl:

here a big house, down the road a shack. They are unaccustomed to this sort of fraternization. Where they live, all the expensive houses are in one area and the more humble dwellings in another. You are either north or south of "the tracks." They have restrictive covenants and zoning laws to enforce this segregation. In Maine, the summer colonies inhabited by people "from away" are also sometimes organized on this basis.

In the country there is more room and more tolerance. If a man has a bigger house than his neighbors, no one cares, and if he has one that is smaller, he's just as welcome. I'd not like it if somebody hauled in an old trailer across the road from me, and then proceeded to collect disintegrating cars, and heave his trash out of his windows, but if it was just a little house that the owners kept tidy, it wouldn't distress me a bit.

We have some extremes hereabouts. At one end of our town a man built a pretty fancy house. I have heard various estimates of the cost (ranging from a million to three million dollars), which, even with inflation and all that, about equals the national debt in the minds of our local citizenry. However, apart from curiosity, which has subsided because the owner was smart enough to have a couple of parties and invite everybody in town to come and take a look, after a few months nobody seemed very interested. All I have ever heard said was, "Well, it'll help with the taxes." True, the owner of the big house can't see any other houses, good or bad, because he is at the end of a lane running down to the shore. However, a few yards along the road from his boundary is about the most astonishing piece of architecture I have ever been privileged to see. The million-dollar man sees it every time he leaves his property, but I don't think it bothers him. So far as I know, the people who own it are decent, respectable folk, even if they did not hire I.M. Pei as their architect and me as their landscape designer.

When I was a little spryer than I have come to be of late, I used to walk almost every day to Naskeag Harbor. It was a comfortable walk—about three-and-a-half miles round trip. On my way I passed a house owned and occupied by a friendly neighbor, who had a little white dog. Whenever I walked by, the dog ran out and barked. Then one day it decided sterner measures were needed. It bit me. I was not hurt—at least not from the bite, which was only a pinch—but I *was* hurt because I had not been able to convince the dog I was a nice, friendly, dog-loving fellow. My neighbor was embarrassed and said he would keep Fido in the house from then on. I said not to do it. The next time I passed, the dog bit me again. This time he tore a triangular hole in my pants. I told my friend I didn't mind being bitten, as that would heal, but that pants cost money. I didn't see the dog again, so I guess it was brought indoors whenever anyone saw me coming.

This is kind of a long way around to tell you about my neighbor's house, the one that didn't cost a million dollars. It must suit him all right, because he has lived in it for thirty years, to my knowledge, but architecturally it looks a bit like a muskrat's nest that has seen a bad winter. It has the usual assortment of parts for this and that lying around outside and I am sure would horrify anyone from the Health and Welfare establishment. But one should not judge from appearances. My friend is quite happy, and I am sure would not want to live anywhere else—and I would not want him to, because he is a good neighbor. He lives as he wants to live and so do I. (If everyone felt as we do, there would be less strife in the world.) I noticed the other day that he had erected a bluebird's box on top of a long swaying pole that leans as his house does. I'll bet you he gets a tenant promptly next spring.

Gazing at Isle au Haut

WHEN I CAME to Amen Farm to live, what is now my lawn and flower garden west of the house was a piece of rough ground encumbered with half-a-dozen decaying frame buildings. One of them was a chicken house, or at least that is what I called it, because there were two hens of indeterminate ancestry pecking about within its broken, rusty wire enclosure. What the other buildings had been I do not know, but I solved the problem by bulldozing them all together and setting a match to them.

During the next few years we "ploughed the fields and scattered the good seed on the land," as the old hymn instructs us, and picked out the assorted rocks and hardware. Its actual transformation into a garden did not come until later, when we surrounded it with what is now a ten-foot-tall cedar hedge and planted a copper beech in the center, four flowering crabs toward the corners, and a flower border in front of the cedars.

Before the hedge was planted, obstructing my path, I could walk about a third of a mile to the top corner of my hayfield. I remember a picnic we once had there, building a fire in front of a boulder to broil the chicken. In those days, I could stand and see the whole of the top of Isle au Haut to the south. Today, because of the growth of the firs and spruces on my own and my neighbor's land, I have to climb on top of the boulders in order to even glimpse the peak of the island's highest point. My old reliable American Guide series, a project of the WPA, says the altitude of the peak is 556 feet, but the U.S. Coast and Geodetic Survey says 543. Being a resident, I am going to stick with the WPA even though it was among the first of the alphabetical rabbits that spawned the thousands of unintelligible assortments of letters inflicted upon us by governments worldwide.

In those early days I used to sit there on my rock and gaze at the top of Isle au Haut, some thirteen miles away. For some reason I am not sure of, that corner of the field was never cleared of rocks, although the trees and brush were kept down, the result being that it is overgrown by juniper and blueberries (the junipers are winning) and is not much good for anything except meditating. However, I don't think of that exercise as nonproductive, and am pretty sure that if there were more of it, the world would be a better place. I don't get there as often now, because walking that far across a rough field is more difficult. I also seem to be less well-adapted physically to meditation on rocks than I used to be. I do wander there occasionally, though, and there is no more pleasant look-out on a still day in the early autumn, when the fragrance of the junipers, combined with the flavor of a sparse handful of wild blueberries, serves notice that this is the time of the annual maturing of nature.

I wonder why people don't take more time to enjoy themselves as they pass through life. One of my books is called A Countryman's Journal. The title was chosen by the publishers over my own, which was

"Take Time to Smell the Flowers." I agree that their title is probably more specific and will, I hope, sell more books, but what I was trying to convey in my title was a concern that we should take more joy of the road we travel. Too many of us spend our lives like Thoreau's farmer, "pushing before us a barn seventy-five feet by forty, its Augean stables never cleansed, and one hundred acres of land, tillage, mowing, pasture and woodlot!" If you protest that your employment is too demanding to allow time to "smell the flowers," I will tell you that to do so takes no time at all. You do not have even to sit on a rock for ten minutes and gaze at distant Isle au Haut: you can accomplish what you need merely by thinking about what you are looking at as you travel about your lawful occasions. It is a matter of habit.

I leave you with a story credited to the poet Southey, who said he knew a man who always put on his spectacles when he ate cherries so they might look larger and more tempting. I shall not labor the point, as I think you can carry it forward from there.

Being Rich

OH WAD SOME POWER THE GIFTIE GIE US

TO SEE OURSELS AS OTHERS SEE US!

IT WAD FRAE MONIE A BLUNDER FREE US,

AN FOOLISH NOTION.

—ROBERT BURNS

I don't know who Robbie Burns had in mind when he wrote the foregoing but I never thought it applied to me. I was sure I was seen as a quiet, reasonably friendly fellow, who paid his bills on time and was indistinguishable from other citizens, except for spending more time than most on gardening and being a bit soft in the head about books.

While I don't have any particular money problems, it never occurred to me that people thought me wealthy, except that, like Petulengro, I am always bragging about owning "night and day, brother, both sweet things; sun, moon, and stars, brother, all sweet things; there's likewise a wind on the heath," but these can't be cashed at the teller's window.

This cozy picture of myself was shattered the other day by a young man of forty-five who came from Boston to interview me about a recent book. He probably didn't think he was young, but I did. When you are ninety, anybody under fifty seems practically in swaddling clothes. I mention his age because maybe it had something to do with how he saw me. His report of the interview was accurate and friendly. He didn't say much about the book, but allowed I was a "pretty good country writer," though sort of overshadowed by E.B. White, who lived in the same town, which is about how I view myself. I haven't anything to complain about, but I am interested that the thing making the greatest impression on him was my "wealth." I have always known my neighbors could see I was reasonably well-off financially, but I thought it a matter of minor importance, and I guess it is to people who see me rather than my surroundings. Cold-turkey, to a stranger, the ambience won out.

In his column my visitor mentioned being admitted by a "housekeeper," and thought he saw my "gardener" through the window. I guess Nancy *is* our housekeeper, but somehow or other I don't see her that way. Five days a week, in the mornings, she keeps us tidied up, but she also happens to be one of our town's three selectmen, and to us she is a friendly neighbor who gives us a hand—a part of the family. After all, when you are our age you need a little help around the place, whether you pay for it or are lucky enough to have family to do it for free. The "gardener" was Ivar, Nancy's husband, who does what I did myself up to a few years ago, when I found that chasing bulls and rams, and doing all the other jobs needed to keep a "farm" operating, was a bit too much for me. It is true that Ivar gardens, but he does many other things, from building airplanes in his cellar to decapitating chickens—and he can mix a mean martini.

A couple of days later I had my reviewer's opinion confirmed, but with a twist that made me feel warm inside. A neighbor stopped by to see me. My other housekeeper, my wife, answered the door (the kitchen door, for that is the only one we ever use) and told me that Gary wanted to speak to me. He said that he had nothing special to see me about, but just wanted to let me know that he had enjoyed my book very much and was reading it to the kids in his English class. They liked it too, but what made me happy was that he added, "I've known you around here for a good many years. I guess I just thought of you as being rich—having a bit more than the rest of us—but I never really knew you until I read your book. I feel differently now."

Robbie Burns was right: knowing how others see us would indeed "frae monie a blunder free us, an foolish notion." Maybe we don't work hard enough at trying to find out.

Time

WHEN MY WIFE and I were on our way to have lunch with friends the other day, we stopped to empty our mailbox. In addition to the usual clutch of catalogues there was just one letter. Helen said, "It's from a Mrs. Greene. I don't know any Greene—do you?" I answered that I did not, and that it was probably fan mail. "No," said my wife, "it's addressed to both of us." "Well," I responded, "let's open it. There's no point in trying to guess who it is from the outside of the envelope."

I was surprised and pleased to find it was from a young lady (at least, she had been young then) whose wedding I had attended forty years ago. I had known her since she was a child, and we had developed a mutual affection. After her wedding and reception she kissed me good-bye and walked out of my life. I never saw her again, only heard of her indirectly, and had no idea of her whereabouts. How she came to find me now is not a part of this story, but I am delighted she has. It made me think of how one's life becomes compartmented.

As the world has developed during the twentieth century, society has become ever more mobile. In my grandparents' time people were commonly born in the same house in which their parents had first drawn breath. Often several generations, even if they did not live in the same house, resided for the most part in or near the same village or town. They continued throughout their lives an acquaintance with the same people, whether related or not. Some few went off to foreign parts, but they were the exceptions, and were remembered on holidays and reunions. In those days, if I had gone to a wedding forty years earlier, I would have grown old watching the bride and groom mature and have children and grandchildren. There would have been a continuing community of interest. The thread would never have been broken. I would have grieved at their sorrows and shared their joys. They, in turn, would have shared my grief and happiness. In those days if one was cut, all bled. There are people who say it was a provincial and busybody society; perhaps to a degree it was—but the rewards were great.

In these latter days, our lives have been chopped into sections. Continuity has been sacrificed to "progress," whatever that is. I count my own life as an example. In all the long years of it I have met many people, made some friends, lost others, and lived and worked in different places. People have moved in and out of my life, some without a trace, others leaving a fragrant memory, but there are none with whom my whole life has been contemporaneous.

In memory, my correspondent is still young and pretty, about twenty, and stepping wide-eyed into an unknown and fascinating world. Though I shall be most happy to see her again, I wonder what I shall find. Will the same person be there, or will forty years have wrought such changes as to make recognition impossible? I am not thinking of physical changes, as these are inevitable. I wonder what has happened to the blithe spirit I knew. What happens to all of us as the years roll by? Some souls there are who defy time, who are but burnished by it; others are indelibly marked by the blast of the years. Four hundred years ago Thomas Watson said,

> TIME WASTETH YEARS, MONTHS, AND HOURS,
> TIME DOTH CONSUME FAME, HONOR, WIT AND STRENGTH,
> TIME KILLS THE GREENEST HERBS AND SWEETEST FLOWERS,
> TIME WEARS OUT YOUTH AND BEAUTY'S LOOKS AT LENGTH,
> TIME DOTH CONVEY TO GROUND BOTH FOE AND FRIEND,
> AND EACH THING ELSE BUT LOVE, WHICH HATH NO END.

What I think a continuing close community affords is shelter from the wasting of the years. We are, in these latter days, like Horace, who complained, "Where the storm drives me I turn for shelter." We no longer make our lives, they are made for us by constantly changing circumstances, but one thing still resists time. It is, as Watson said, love, indestructible, all-powerful, all-embracing, all-sheltering.

Eternity

ONE OF THE MANY advantages of living on the coast of Maine is that our way of life allows us a few spare moments to think of things beyond the immediate. There is not the push and hurry, and the "much ado about nothing" that pervades urban areas. I took advantage of this freedom recently to read a book entitled *Life Itself, Its Origin and Nature*. It was written by Francis Crick, the Nobel Prize–winning biologist. His book is about biology, the origin of life, and the origin of man. There is also a little science fiction for those who have a liking for such imaginings.

I realize "origin of life" and "origin of man" are fighting words to TV evangelists and those who think as they do, but there are a great many people who do not think as they do, who are able to live comfortably with both science and religion. It is with this group I count myself, and I should like to examine the subject without passion.

I am sure fundamentalists will believe me consigned to Hell, and scientists will shake their heads in sorrow over a man willing to believe without proof.

The creationist vs. evolutionist controversy was settled legally by federal judge William Overton, when he found unconstitutional an Arkansas law requiring the Biblical story of creation to be taught alongside the theory of evolution, as a science. As might be expected, no change has come about in the convictions held by the fundamentalists. They still believe that God began work on the morning of the first day and had the job of creation completed so that he "rested on the seventh day from all His work He had made." They reject all material findings to the contrary, resting their case on an unshakable belief that the Bible is not only a work of spiritual guidance but a revealed document of such accuracy that it overrides all scientific evidence that does not accord with it.

Evolutionists, having no Bible to hamper them, go ahead on the evidence, and since the sole aim of science is to seek out truth, make some compelling arguments. Mr. Crick and his fellows theorize that one day, eight or ten billion years ago (it doesn't really matter when), there was a hell of a big bang out there in the wild blue yonder, and all the universe began to fall into place. If this stretches your mind a bit, consider that it is certainly no more unlikely than that an anthropomorphic god put together in a week the whole universe and its occupants, including but not limited to (as a lawyer would say) forty thousand species of spiders and a few billion bacteria.

Both theories posit a point at which time began, when it is quite obvious that there has never been any beginning, just as there will never be any end. It is almost impossible for man, even with his amazing intelligence, to conceive of unlimited space. We think of time passing, whereas (with apologies to Thoreau) it is but the stream in which we go a-fishing. The evolutionists keep one foot on the ground by having the big bang fling out a cloud of dust and gases, but without saying where the cloud originated. The truth is, they do not know and neither does anyone else. They are on surer ground with man, who is a newcomer and has left his spoor behind him. Even earth itself is of comparatively recent origin—a few billion years, what difference?—but time and space, which are, as Einstein said, private to every being, have never *not* been. Who knows? If the scientists are close in the big-bang theory, and they well may be, entire universes have been coming into being and self-destructing forever in the past, and will continue to do so forever in the future. It is only man's finite mind that has to have a beginning and an end.

The most amazing thing that exists is intelligence. It cannot be detected by any of the five senses, but its existence is obvious. Men were trying to define God long before the Christian era. Theologians have used enough paper in this quest to wrap up the world, and every religion that has ever existed has had a crack at it, but the truth is that we will all have to do so for ourselves. I cannot think of God (as do the fundamentalists) as an anthropomorphic deity sitting up on Cloud Nine, zapping the unbelievers and handing out Girl Scout cookies to the righteous; nor can I conceive of him turning off natural laws like gravity in order to impress people. But I am quite convinced there *is* an everlasting intelligence that is far beyond the understanding of human beings.

Whether God can exist without man to know there is a God is something to ponder on. Martin Luther's biographer, Roland Bainton, reports that Luther remarked to Erasmus, "Suppose the world goes to smash! God can make another." That is one way of looking at it. Another is Voltaire's belief that "if God did not exist it would be necessary to invent him." The truth is that there is a duality of God and man, and one cannot exist without the other.

Regardless of how earth and man came into being, the only salvation for man in an increasingly hazardous social environment is the Christian principle. Whether you believe Jesus Christ to be man or God, or both, cuts no mustard; billions of people have never heard of him. What there is no argument about is the shining truth of the Christian ethic. We must cherish it and live up to its philosophy as best we can, and the world, about whose creation there is so much fret and pother, can be our host for millennia. Ignore it, and our time will be brief.

Read, and Meditate

YEARS AGO, WITH the help with another young man (it was long enough ago that I can say another *young* man), I designed a bookplate for my modest library. It is interesting to examine it now, after the passage of fifty years, and to have visible evidence that the star by which I was proposing to guide my life still burns brightly. There have been periods when the continuous necessity of making a living and the events of the world over which I had no control kept me busy about other things, but when I took time to look, the star was always there.

If, switching metaphors, you want to know what was, or for that matter still is that magic talisman, I will quote it:

HOW CALM AND QUIET A DELIGHT
IS IT, ALONE,
TO READ, AND MEDITATE, AND WRITE,
BY NONE OFFENDED, AND
OFFENDING NONE!
TO WALK, RIDE, SIT OR SLEEP
AT ONE'S OWN EASE!
AND, PLEASING A MAN'S SELF,
NONE OTHER TO DISPLEASE.

If you are not familiar with the quotation, you will find it in Isaac Walton's *Compleat Angler*. It was not Walton who wrote it, but his bosom friend and fishing companion Charles Cotton. It is a statement of a tranquil philosophy that has ever fewer adherents in this modern world, where most people seem to believe that *their* way is the best way and their true mission in life is to convert all others, no matter that it may take unbelievable mental and physical cruelty to do so. Of course *all* people are not cruel, but it seems, sadly, that most are unwilling to allow their neighbor to "walk, ride, sit, or sleep at [his] own ease and pleasing [himself], none other to displease."

I saw a fox trotting along the road while I sat at breakfast yesterday. I know not everybody is lucky enough to be able to admire a fox while enjoying his toast and marmalade, and I am grateful. (I interject this to save someone the trouble of writing to tell me I would not be so philosophical if I ate breakfast looking out at an urban jungle.) I think I know where my fox's den is: in a jumble of boulders and brush at the bottom of the shore pasture. It is a very good place for a fox to have its habitation as it is practically impenetrable except to foxes. Reynard came across the field and not up my neighbor's lane, which provides more shelter, because he figured, I think, that there was a better chance on this route of rustling up a mouse or some other tidbit. There was no traffic on the road separating us (there rarely is), but he kept to the side facing the traffic. He dragged his brush behind, as foxes usually do when they are just ambling. I think they use it when they jump, in the same way a high-wire artist uses his pole for balance.

The fox was pleasing himself and not displeasing others, but I am sure if a man with a gun had been nearby he would have shot him. If you asked why, he would probably have told you that foxes carry rabies

A Countryman's Farewell

and steal chickens. The fact that he owned no chickens, and that drunkards driving cars kill more people in a week than rabid foxes do in a hundred years would not impress him. He probably would feel the same way about Democrats or Republicans, Communists or capitalists, black men or white, or anyone who did not think as he did. He would be sure what he believed was right and that everybody who disagreed was wrong and should be shown the light—or shot. He was not a *seeker* after truth; he was sure it had been revealed to him. He would not have echoed Pontius Pilate's words, "What is truth?" (A good question, incidentally. I think Pontius Pilate got some bad press.)

I don't show most people my bookplate, because I would be labeled an old man who has no interest in mankind's welfare and therefore should be ignored. By his injunction Charles Cotton did not mean that we should be selfish and fiddle while Rome burns, but that we should indeed "read, and meditate, and write," and thus have something in our minds above partisan opinion, and admit that we have much to learn.

You will note that Cotton said we should displease and offend none. I don't think I have been wholly successful in that, but I flatter myself that I have tried. Even those with whom I disagree—because they are illogical, and whether or not one is logical is as definite as the angles in an equilateral triangle—I merely avoid. I don't argue with them. It is remarkable how much stress can be bypassed by keeping quiet. Was it not Marcus Aurelius who said one could save a world of trouble by having no opinion on a variety of subjects? I think what he meant was *voicing* an opinion. Any reflective man has opinions, which is why Cotton advocated that one "read, and meditate, and write," but no one is called upon to belabor others with them.

November

NOBODY HAS MUCH to say in praise of November. Sir Walter Scott, in "Marmion," wrote, "November's sky is chill and drear, / November's leaf is red and sear." And though Thomas Hood (whom I don't think much of otherwise) penned: "I saw old autumn in the misty morn / Stand shadowless like silence, listening / To silence," which has a certain pensive charm, he is also responsible for

NO WARMTH, NO CHEERFULNESS, NO HEALTHFUL EASE,
NO COMFORTABLE FEEL IN ANY MEMBER—
NO SHADE, NO SHINE, NO BUTTERFLIES, NO BEES,
NO FRUITS, NO FLOWERS, NO LEAVES, NO BIRDS,
NOVEMBER.

Personally, I don't think November is all that bad. Here in Maine it is more like the tail end of autumn than the chill beginning of winter. Maine springs are nothing to brag about: they advance and retreat every day or so for a couple of months, then all of a sudden it is summer, and the whole garden and countryside burst into exuberant bloom within ten days. Autumn, though, is something else. Down where we live, near salt water, it goes on and on and on. I am writing this on November 4, and the dooryard, though a trifle bedraggled, is bright with pink dahlias and a few chrysanthemums. A visitor was here yesterday to look at the garden and greenhouse, and I took her back to the vegetables, where I was able to find her a perfect, fragrant sweet pea. In case you wonder, I grow my sweet peas in the kitchen garden because they are preeminently for cutting, and a row of sweet peas in a flower garden is a mess.

There is still plenty to eat in the garden. There is a row of leeks as thick around as your wrist—none of those puny little store-bought things that look like overgrown scallions; there are still onions to harvest and a row of Buttercrunch lettuce under *cloche* that we shall be eating until December. We just cut the last of our Romaine, which stood without any protection. (Romaine is a lettuce that should be grown cool, so we plant a late crop in August and enjoy it through October, when the nights have grown cold.)

There have been several minor frosts, thirty degrees was the lowest, but all they did was brown the foliage of the zucchinis, which we were glad to be rid of. (Somehow or other I do not have the moral fortitude to pull up a plant that is still bearing, even if I don't know what to do with its fruit.) Our tomatoes are all indoors, not so much because they would have been frozen, for they were well up off the ground, but because in cold weather they do not fill out and when cut are empty like peppers. They are all in the cold cellar on a table now, a hundred or so of them. They were green when we took them in but are ripening fast. Tomatoes don't need sun to ripen—as a matter of fact, if you place a green tomato on the windowsill in direct sunlight, it is likely to scald before it ripens.

Those unfamiliar with the locality are always surprised to find us picking our last blueberries in November. Not the wild ones, though you can find a few of them if you search long enough, but fruits from our little plot of cultivated high-bush plants. They are high enough off the ground so that the first few frosts do them no harm, and even now the late varieties are still loaded with fruit. The berries are not as sweet as they were when there was more sunshine, but a few days in the house, and a little sugar, will do wonders. We use most of them for pies or cobbler.

I think the old Romans had it about right, because for them November was only the ninth month of the year. They didn't think about a new year until March, and at that time did not have a long winter facing them as we do.

November is hunters' month, so I stay out of the woods, but I can understand the feelings of those who wait anxiously every year for the time they will be spending their days in the thinning woodlands. I am not very keen on shooting deer, but my feelings make no sense so long as I have no objection to slaughtering farm animals for food, and I do not object to that. The hunters do, as they say, "cull" a few deer, and they seem to cull a few of the species Homo sapiens along with them, which may not be all that bad either. Like the deer they are going to die anyway, and I doubt one can measure the pain of being shot against some other swing of the sickle.

WINTER

I crown thee king of intimate delights,
Fireside enjoyments, home-born happiness,
And all the comforts that the lowly roof
Of undisturb'd retirement, and the hours
Of long uninterrupted evening know.
  —from The Task IV, *by William Cowper, 1785*

The Time to Be Happy

THE TIME TO be happy is now. Yesterday is gone, and tomorrow may never come. I was reminded of this as I walked down the lane to a cottage we have on the shore of Blue Hill Bay. During the summer our kids occupy it, but in the winter we keep it boarded up against the storms and take up the steps that lead down the bluff to the beach. To-day was not what one would think of as a "nice" day. Rain was no longer falling, as it had been until recently, but the clouds were still low, and a gusty wind was swaying the tops of the birches, shaking down small showers. The lane was difficult walking, as the heavy rains had torn deep gullies in one spot. I made mental note that next spring I would have to haul in a yard or so of gravel, and dump and drag it.

When I started on my inspection tour I had thought of using the car to ride the hill, but decided against it. I said to myself, Look now, even if it is a hill, you are not so old yet you can't walk half a mile, and so it proved. You can do a lot of things if you don't rush your fences. Walking is always better than riding. You see more. You also hear and feel and are subliminally conscious of more. I think, perhaps, the things you observe without identifying them, things you just feel, are the most important.

What I really wanted to learn was whether or not Carlton had taken up the steps. He had not. He had a job of greater urgency, closing in the house of a friend who had suffered the misfortune of a major fire. While I was anxious that the steps be taken up before snowfall, I was glad when I found them still down, as they afforded me the op-portunity of taking one more walk along the shore before winter set in. Even if you can get to the water's edge in the winter, walking is difficult over and around the ice floes stranded by the high tides.

What made me think the time to be happy was now? Well, several things. In the first place, I had accomplished something I had been dubious about attempting, and we are always gratified by present accomplishment. We may have been very important in mid-life, but that doesn't do much for us when we are old and out of the race. (Muhammed Ali was the center of the ring for years, but that fact won't do much to elevate his spirits when he is eighty.) Walking half a mile down a hill, along a shoreline, and back up again is no big deal, I know. I have done it many times, but as the going gets tougher the sense of achievement gets larger, so even a modest victory pays big dividends. I suppose I got more happiness out of my half mile today than I did out of five miles ten years ago.

The shore was deserted, as it almost always is. There were not even any clam diggers, just a few boats dragging for scallops a mile or so offshore. But there was a stiff, cold wind that I had to lean into to keep my balance. There was salt spray on my lips, and tears ran from the corners of my eyes. The sea was not in its summer garb of whitecapped blue but showed a dirty gray, discolored by the silt churned up from the bottom. There were streaks of foam where the wind whipped froth before it. I struggled along until I could shelter in the lee of a huge boulder that had tumbled out of the bluff in a winter storm some years back. I was grateful for the shelter, to get my breath. I rested against the cold granite while I buttoned my coat. It was like being stayed by the bulk of the world.

When I started back I was hurried by the force of the gale, now behind me. I walked balancing back against the wind, like a woman far gone in pregnancy, watching my footing amidst the rocks. The steps, when I reached them, were steeper than I remembered and I had to rest before I climbed, but I felt renewed in spirit. As I labored slowly back uphill—fifty paces and a rest, fifty paces and a rest—I had time to admire and enjoy the chalky bark of the birches. Here and there in the grove stood a few young spruces that will, in another score of years, turn the graceful white woodland into a somber green, but now it was still open, with wild roses bright with red hips and clumps of holly, almost stripped of their berries by the migrating birds, providing the undergrowth. I saw, too, that the young alders were sprouting again, reminding me of my constant battle against them.

When I reached the house I found friend Gail, who makes our Christmas wreaths for us, busily fastening them to the picket fence surrounding our dooryard. There were thirteen wreaths in all, eleven on the fence and one on the front door (which no one ever uses), and the other welcoming the visitor to the kitchen. There was even a bow and some greenery on the mailbox. Now, I said to myself, is the time to be happy.

Christmas

SPEAKING OF OLD age, Edith Wharton is said to have remarked, "The only thing to do is to hug our friends tight—and do one's job." I believe this is true whether one is old or young. Friends are not easily come by, and those we have should be viewed as we see great treasures.

I am brought to this consideration of friendship because of the presence of the Christmas season. Christmas is, of course, a religious observance, a celebration of the birth of the founder of the Christian faith; but it is more than that, because many who have little, if any, belief in Christ are nonetheless moved by the spirit of Christmas. It has come to be a celebration of love and friendship, and even though commercialized and vulgarized, its underlying virtue shines through to help us all to be kinder people.

I copy out of my commonplace book a note that I made some time ago: "He is not rich that possesses much, but he that covets no more," which is another way of expressing Thoreau's belief that one could be rich by not wanting too much. This is the secret of happiness. Most of us, I believe, are more grateful for modest Christmas gifts evidencing thoughtfulness than we are for things expensive but not from the heart. Sadly, in recent years, Christmas has become more of a spectacle and less of a gentle remembrance of love and affection.

It is easy to succumb to commercial inducements whose primary purpose is to increase sales, but at the same time it becomes more difficult to do something individual for each person. Not everyone is a reader, but for those who are, books are the answer. I am not sure about books being small gifts nowadays, but at least they are not ostentatious, and they are personal and keep on giving.

The real gifts of Christmas, though, are small tokens of love and remembrance. When I was young (here I go writing about myself again) not much *money* was spent on gifts, but a good deal of time was devoted to making, or rummaging around to find, small things suitable to the individual. I can remember, as a child, cleaning out walnut shells, gilding the outside, and lining them with silk or velvet to hold a small silver coin especially polished for the occasion. Just as in John

Leech's illustrations for Charles Dickens's *A Christmas Carol*, we tucked evergreens behind the picture frames and hung mistletoe and holly from the chandelier. In those quieter days, the ladies of the family gave scarves or shawls they had knitted or crocheted, embroidered handkerchiefs, gloves, or perhaps boxes of note paper, calendars, or even a sheet of two-cent postage stamps. (Two cents was all it cost then to send a domestic letter. I have a little folding calendar, just three by four inches, called "A Pansy Calendar," which is delightfully decorated with pansy faces. It is from the year 1888 and lists the holidays, eclipses, and other data for that year. It also states that you can "send a letter to all civilized countries, with a few exceptions, for 5¢.")

I still read *A Christmas Carol* every year, and do so from a facsimile copy of the original edition given me as a present long ago. It cost only two dollars and was published by the Atlantic Monthly Press, which exhorted the potential purchaser to "buy two copies of it, one to give away and one to read." My copy is particularly meaningful to me because A. Edward Newton—a great bibliophile and a fellow member of the Art Club of Philadelphia—wrote on a fly page, "I still am of the opinion that this is the Greatest Little Book in the World."

Flower books were favorites for Christmas giving. Before me is one for 1913 called *The Language of Flowers*, reprinted in 1971 and (as far as I know) still available.

In the nineteenth century, new flower books were published every year. The most famous of all was J.J. Grandville's *Les fleurs animées*. This was published in Paris in 1867 and then republished in England, Germany, and the United States (pirated probably) many times thereafter. I have ten or a dozen little flower books, all called *The Language of Flowers* or *Flower Sentiments* or something of that nature. People also gave little tussy-mussies of real flowers for Christmas, perhaps snowdrops that had been forced, or a few holly and mistletoe sprigs surrounded with a frill of lace. The whole essence of the thing was that the gift should be small and personal. Expensive gifts would have been embarrassing. By today's standards nobody except the very rich had much money, but most people were able to make Christmas a joyous holiday just because money did not have much to do with it. It was a time for remembering old friends and, as Mrs. Wharton said, hugging them tight.

Jane Austen

I RECENTLY BOUGHT a book I recommend to you. It is about Jane Austen.* I guess you might well wonder why another book about her is needed. I wondered too—which is why I bought it. I am glad I did, because after reading it I am satisfied it is a substantial addition to the Jane Austen *oeuvre*. Lord David Cecil, the author, has provided all dedicated Janeites with a more rounded illumination of the world she lived in and wrote about than they had previously possessed. It will also provide, for those who have not read Jane Austen, a surer foundation for understanding her novels. The foreword posits a point upon which the book rests:

> I have taken particular pains to set my heroine in the context of the period and society in which she lived. My reason for this is that I have come across critics who discuss her and her view of life and character as if they were those of a contemporary of their own. The result is a portrait comically misleading. For, as we should have learned both from social historians and common observation, we are all largely the creatures of the world we happen to have been born into and our outlook is conditioned by its assumptions and beliefs and conventions and customs.

David Cecil's observation is correct. We *are* all fashioned by the times and places of our birth, and by the customs then and there prevailing. Most Americans are Christians—card-carrying members or just nominal—but the only reason we are is because we were born in a country where the Christian religion is dominant. We made no choice, and if we had been born in Iran we would have been Muslims, or in China, Buddhists; which is why occasionally I am impatient with those who are sure they have the only working hot-line to God. There are, you know, only about a billion Christians, and about four billion people of other faiths or no faith at all. It has always puzzled me what Christians, particularly the born-again variety, are going to do about

*A *Portrait of Jane Austen*, by David Cecil. London: Constable, 1978.

these "lesser breeds without the law," as Kipling called them in his "Recessional." If you have to believe in Jesus Christ and be reborn to get into heaven, I guess there must be a lot of second-class accommodations for the non-Christians.

But to get back to Jane Austen. Her novels may seem stilted to modern readers accustomed to casual English and the uninhibited use of Anglo-Saxon four-letter words, but Jane lived in a different era. This fact does not mean the underlying motivation of people was different, only that they were better disciplined in their particular way of life, and certainly better disciplined in talking about it. That she was a genius working in miniature, no one competent to judge would deny. Jane Austen painted *in little* and never stepped outside her experience, showing by her restraint that in addition to being a nice observer of life around her, she was an intelligent writer who knew her limitations as well as her abilities.

In addition to being a biography, *A Portrait of Jane Austen* devotes much attention to the class structure prevailing in her time, something the reader needs to know in order to fully appreciate her novels. As I have mentioned before, England was then—and still is—a singularly class-structured society. The unwillingness of labor to enter into comfortable accommodation with management (who, in labor's view, represent the upper classes) is at the heart of much of England's economic troubles. It has looked for some time as though the venerable *Times* of London would sooner or later fall victim to this ancient feud. Although the class system is pervasive, it is much more virulent in urban and industrial areas than in the country.

A *social* class system is almost impossible for an American to understand. We have an *economic* class structure, and so does every country, but that is different; it is not passed on in the blood and distinguishable by accent. I know rather more than most people about the subject, because I lived in England for years as a young American sitting in the bleachers, watching but not being part of the game. To enjoy Jane Austen you must know something of what it was like in the eighteenth and early nineteenth centuries. Lord David Cecil's book will give you a few pointers.

"The Milk"

WHEN I OPENED the kitchen door this morning to bring in the milk, I found a sheet of paper under the carton, addressed to "Dear Customer." It didn't say very much, just that, due to the rising cost of gasoline and maintenance of the trucks, home deliveries were being discontinued. They hoped that thereafter we would buy their products at any store of our choice.

While I suppose I shall not be inconvenienced very much, as I have to shop for other things anyway, I was saddened by this decision, for it represents the loss of just one more personal contact between provider and consumer. I shall miss the sound of the milk truck coming around the corner by the barn and pulling up alongside the kitchen door. I guess I am growing old and don't like change. The arrival of "the milk" about six every morning was a dependable and predictable prelude to the day's affairs. Our dogs regularly bark at all strange cars, but the sound of the milk truck was a part of their lives, and the only recognition they gave it was to cock an ear and open an eye. No matter what the weather, "the milk" never failed. On winter mornings when the drive had not yet been plowed and was still under two feet of snow, the heavy truck negotiated it without trouble.

Had I been asked, I would willingly have paid a little more to maintain the service. I regret the passing of old customs, but I suppose most people would not, or perhaps could not, afford to pay more. Everything nowadays is becoming so computerized and impersonal that even so small a thing as the loss of the milkman's daily visit makes me unhappy. There used to be "the fish," "the ice," "the bread," and half a dozen other more or less regular callers, but about the only one left now is the mail, and from trial balloons I see floating above Washington, I doubt *that* will continue much longer either.

When I was younger, and not so very much younger, milk was delivered in glass bottles closed with a little cardboard disk carrying the name of the dairy. If the milk had stood a while, the first thing we did after bringing it in was to pour off "the top of the bottle." This of course was in the days before homogenization foiled such larceny. When homogenized milk first appeared I thought it a pretty good idea, but

I soon changed my mind. I found I no longer had any "top of the bottle" to stir into my coffee or pour on my blueberries, but instead had to buy cream from the dairy. Of course, in the old days when I stole from the milk for my coffee, I was left with skimmed milk to drink, but I doubt it did me any great harm. In fact, it may have been good for me.

During the winter, the cold acted as a separator. After a good frosty night, the cardboard disk was elevated on a pillar of frozen cream two inches high. All one had to do was to pry it off into a pitcher. We once owned a small dog (to be truthful, he owned us, as most dogs own those with whom they live) who, if he was let out on a frosty morning, delighted in licking the frozen cream protruding from the milk bottle. Nicknamed Lanky, he was a Scottish terrier of royal pedigree. His real name was Lord Lancaster of Rivanel, and his ancestry, beside which mine was *parvenu*, stretched back into the days of Robert the Bruce. He also plucked tomatoes warm from the vine and after one bite left them on the ground.

But I digress.

Besides not having all that much enthusiasm for homogenization, I am not overly happy about pasteurized milk. I realize the need for it when milk is collected, as it is, from many different farms and shipped around in tank trucks as though it were something made in a factory rather than being the lactic fluid of a warm-blooded animal like ourselves, but to anyone accustomed to raw milk, the pasteurized variety tastes like caramel custard.

For a good many years we kept a family cow or two at Amen Farm, usually Guernseys, and always had a pitcher of milk and another of cream in the milk-room refrigerator. It was bovine nectar. I drank a lot of milk, and it has, apparently, not shortened my life. The cream, which we used freely, poured like cold molasses and frightened our dieting guests, who thought it would plug up their arteries, but we seem to have survived it. Of course our cows were regularly tested for tuberculosis and brucellosis, and as they were never exposed to other cattle, or humans other than ourselves, the chance of infection was minimal. I would suppose that since tuberculosis among humans has been so markedly reduced in recent years, there will be less among cattle. A veterinarian friend once told me that he thought more cows caught tuberculosis from humans than humans did from cows.

So it seems "the milk" will not be waking me in the morning, and since I no longer have any cows in the barn, I shall like most citizens have to buy my milk at the store, but I guess it will be the same milk. Somebody will be up in the dark of mornings to milk somebody's cows, so things won't change much. *Plus ça change, plus c'est la même chose.*

Libraries

I HAVE BEEN thinking about books. Not unusual for me because my life, even in its stressful periods, has been warmed by books and by the companionship of other book-lovers, living and dead. I have been thinking about them particularly today because I spent the afternoon at the Searsport Library. It is not a large library but it is typical of many like it all across the populated parts of New England. The people who settled this less than entirely hospitable part of the Western world had a great respect for scholarship; and where does learning begin except in a library, where you can hold in your hands the accumulated knowledge of those who have gone before? By picking up at the point where their parents struggled to arrive, each succeeding generation does not have to start again at the beginning. I sometimes wonder if we who use them (and those who only pass by) appreciate our many libraries. I am not thinking of the great collections of books in nationally known institutions, without which our past would be but a terra incognita, but the hundreds of small oases to be found in almost every village across the country.

In my own town of Brooklin is the Friend Memorial Library, a collection of some thirteen thousand volumes that has, as long as I have lived here, doubled as the school library. Then number of kids who have read their assignments and chewed on their pencils at its tables over the years is beyond counting. The librarians have known who they were, their family problems or advantages, their strengths and weaknesses, and have acted as volunteer teachers. The library was privately founded and endowed in 1900 and has occupied its present building since 1912, being supported by the town and many individual givers.

The Carver Memorial Library in Searsport, housed in an impressive boulder stone building, is just another such institution. Appropriately enough, it was created by a ship's captain (where would Searsport be without its heritage of ships?) whose name it bears. There are similar libraries in almost every hamlet along the coast. In nearby Sedgwick and Sargentville are libraries housed in small buildings hardly large enough to hold a set of the *Encyclopedia Britannica*, testifying to some early citizen's love of learning; for learning is, after all, what libraries are all about.

All my life I have been blessed with books. By the time I was six years old I was an omnivorous reader, and I was so fortunate as to grow up in a house where, like my own today, there were books on the shelves, books on the stairs, books on the floor, and everywhere else that space was available. There was also a village library (the gift of some beneficent landowner) to which I had access.

Other small libraries, very small libraries indeed, have broadened my education and helped me while away the hour. They were the libraries were placed aboard ships by the American Merchant Marine Library Association. The traveling librarian would come aboard with a box of books and take back the ones carried on the previous voyage. The box returned always seemed to be lacking a few books; however, I guess a certain amount of attrition was accepted as being the price of good deeds. The AMMLA introduced me to such disparate writers as Joseph Conrad and Charles Lamb, for which blessings I have stood in their debt for sixty years.

As a writer I have my own home library, which is now pushing six thousand volumes. I could not work without it, not only because of the many reference books it contains, but because it takes me back at the turning of a page to the thoughts of men who were the intellectual companions of my youth. Just recently I have reread Christopher Morley's *Letters of Askance*, which I bought in 1933 but have not touched for many a year. What surprised me was to see that several little tricks of expression I thought were my own were plucked from his vineyard. (Only God could tell you where Morley got them.) It is not that writers steal from one another, but that a reader who is *simpatico* receives an impression like that on sensitized photographic film, and the expression or idea becomes a part of his way of thought.

Most librarians in small towns are women, usually young women, who work part time. As the libraries are open only at stated hours, it would be expensive and unnecessary to employ full-time librarians. Besides, a part-time job is just what some people want. Many of these librarians are fully qualified, but having married or made some other similarly hazardous decision after graduation, they find a part-time job made to order. I hear frequently from librarians who write offering help when I state I am unable to find something. They are uniformly helpful and gracious—and, I am sure, always pretty, though I never see most of them. Some become pen-pals and others stop at Amen Farm to see what I look like. Something sets them apart from the ordinary run of reader. It must be they are intelligent as well as pretty. Not, I hasten to add, that other readers are not intelligent, but being intelligent *and* pretty is quite a trick. (How did I get myself in *that* bind?)

Westmorland

THIS BEING THE New Year, somebody thought to ask me what I had found to write about every week for twenty-two years. I answered that I wrote about what I saw and heard. I do not *make* things up, though I may *mix* them up. Anyone's memory is a rag-bag of recollections, and the older one gets, the fuller is the bag. My difficulty is not so much finding something about which to write, as making a selection, and *that* is usually determined by passing events that trigger an idea.

Sometimes I go over my diary, which I have kept most of my life. Except for a hiatus of about six years, I have a complete run from 1943. I think a good editor might make an interesting book or two out of them, but I would prefer that it was after I am dead, for a diary is where one goes to confess one's sins.

Once, years ago, when I was on a working visit to England (with my wife along as usual), I stole a few days' holiday and drove up to Westmorland. There were two places we particularly wanted to see. One was Beatrix Potter's house in Sawrey, and the other was Dove Cottage, in Grassmere, where William and Dorothy Wordsworth lived during the first years of the nineteenth century. The weather was sunny and beautiful, and, as it is often rainy around the lakes, we revelled in these surroundings we had so often read about.

Most people think of Beatrix Potter in connection with Flopsy, Mopsy, Cottontail, and Peter, but she was a most delicate and sensitive artist who did many other things besides paint appealing little animals. She made wonderfully detailed renderings of bees, bats, birds, and butterflies, and a whole series of paintings of British fungi. If you have enjoyed her children's books and would like to know more about her, I suggest you consider buying *The Journal of Beatrix Potter*, *The Art of Beatrix Potter*, and *The Tale of Beatrix Potter*, all published by Frederick Warne and Company. These are books you will want to keep and read many times. *The Art of Beatrix Potter* contains a vast number of her drawings and watercolors, as well as photographs of her home in Sawrey, a small, low-ceilinged cottage (which I shall always remember, because I took my wife's picture sitting in Beatrix Potter's armchair).

Beatrix Potter died in Sawrey an old lady, in 1943. In her youth she had been a beautiful girl, but was no less memorable as a somewhat crotchety, eccentric old woman in her later years. She loved the hill country and its flocks, and did much to guide those lovely verdant dales into the protection of the National Trust. Almost her last words were written to an old friend and shepherd: "Dear Joe Moscrop . . . Still some strength in me. I write a line to shake you by the hand, our friendship has been entirely pleasant. I am very ill with bronchitis. With best wishes for the New Year. . . ." She died on December 22, 1943, at the age of seventy-seven.

But you see what happens. I did not plan to write about Beatrix Potter at all. When I drove to Blue Hill yesterday, I saw a trail of smoke blowing from the chimney of North Brooklin's "Dove Cottage" (for that is the name I gave the house because it was once owned by Margaret Dove), and I decided to write another essay about it.

I am happy to report that North Brooklin's Dove Cottage has been bought by a young couple who are giving it a new lease on life, modernizing the house without spoiling it, and returning it to its charm of 150 years ago. I saw it while the paneling had been moved in the living room, and the great central chimney stood exposed, as solid and massive as when it was built; the wisp of smoke I saw yesterday certified to its present use. Barring manmade disasters, the cottage will continue to shelter and make secure generations of owners still unborn.

From Dove Cottage my memory took me back to Dorothy Wordsworth. If you have not read her diary, you have missed a great deal. The *Grassmere Journal* covers the years between 1800 and 1803, and is as charming and unposed and as delicate and sensitive as Beatrix Potter's watercolors. Dorothy Wordsworth's journals were edited by E. de Selincourt and published by Macmillan and Company in 1941. They are in two volumes and extend from 1798 until 1828.

Dorothy Wordsworth was an extremely sensitive person, completely devoted to her brother William. Many people believe she was a finer poet and was William's inspiration. How that may be is unimportant to the reader of her journals. What matters is her own simplicity and charm, which glow on every page.

Magazines

THIS HOUSEHOLD RECEIVES a lot of periodical literature, most of which I am ashamed to say I never look at. I am ashamed because it is wasteful to pay for something one has no time to read. I have thought several times that the thing to do would be to drop everything as the renewals come due, but I never quite maintain my determination. What happens is that I pick up the most recent copy, find something in it I like, and say to myself, Oh well, let's give it a try just one more year—maybe I'll have more time to read. The truth is, of course, that I have less time to read because everything I do, including reading, takes longer. I used to go through two or three books, the large with the small, in a week. Now I am lucky to finish one. Being able to read and comprehend quickly, making judgments as you go along, is one of life's greatest pleasures, for with that ability you can look inside another person's head. I can still do it by working hard, but it is not so much fun; it takes a long time, and is done with a hammer and chisel, whereas it used to be a flyby. Magazines can be got through in less time than it takes to read a book, so the temptation is to hang on to certain favorite issues of, for instance, *Down East* and *Reader's Digest*, along with a few others.

Magazines, of course, are not books, though many of our famous nineteenth-century novels were first published in magazines as serials. Even today, much nonfiction follows that road. E.B. White's *One Man's Meat* is an outstanding example. It is difficult for an essayist not to want to leave something more permanent behind than a file of brittle, yellowing newspaper clippings. To do so, though, one must write about less ephemeral things than politics, which somehow or other get into most columnists' lucubrations. The subject must be tied into the eternal small but ageless interests of life. A hundred years from now few people are going to want to read some reporter's revelations about Watergate, but Charles Lamb's "Dissertation upon Roast Pig" or E.B. White's "Death of a Pig" will be read with amusement and understanding five hundred years in the future, if anybody is left alive to read them.

If I were compelled to limit my magazines drastically, one I would keep would be an English publication called *Country Life*. I have been a subscriber for about forty years and have at least a thousand copies in the attic, which I am fearful some day will come crashing down through the ceiling. Now, don't think of me so pityingly—more ceilings have been cracked by piles of *National Geographic* in the attic than by slippage of the San Andreas fault. *Country Life's* pages are filled (as they should be, with such a title) with country articles of the kind that can be read with pleasure at any time. The only difference between a copy dated 1940 and one dated 1980 is in the art work. A gentleman named Ian Niall writes a column in *Country Life* vaguely resembling mine, and he does it every week as I do. He is either the third or fourth writer to hold the job during the years I have been subscribing, and all have been excellent.

The second magazine I would continue is *The Countryman*. (You can see where my interests lie.) This is a quarterly compendium of both current and nostalgic stories, mostly nonfiction, plus a meandering editorial about trends in farming and country matters in England, and how they may be affected by their government—which apparently has the same penchant for bossing people around as ours. *The Countryman* is the size of *Reader's Digest*, only not so obese, and is printed on matte paper. I often carry it around in my pocket so I can improve the shining hour when I tire and have to sit down. I did not discover *The Country-man* until 1949, when I bought a copy in the Monument Station of the London Underground.

Helen says to me, "Why don't you give all those magazines away? You'll never read them again." I reply indignantly, "I shall so. Anyway, I want the garden articles for my writing." (Confidentially, I rarely do turn to them again.)

Coming back to the United States, where there are no magazines of the same country type available (which is just as well as I would probably buy them), there is a journal I would keep—come the holo-caust. This is the *American Scholar*, a publication of Phi Beta Kappa. *American Scholar* is an intellectual journal that for the most part is far above my head, but it serves as a sort of drillmaster telling me, when I read it, to think more clearly and write more thoughtfully; it cheers me, occasionally, to see that even the intelligentsia sometimes hit their thumbs. I bought it initially because the lead article was written by René Dubos, a remarkably interesting and lucid writer. Out of the half-dozen leading articles in each issue, I am usually able to understand, and read, a couple.

These three I would keep. The rest I think I'll allow to expire—maybe.

Beyond Eighty

A FRIEND SUGGESTED I review a recently published book called *The View from Eighty*. I couldn't lay my hands on it at the time, so made a guess and wrote an essay about what I felt sure a book with that title must concern itself with. I have since read it and can recom-mend it to you. It is published by Viking Press, New York, and the author, Malcolm Cowley, is one of that select band of citizens who are octogenarians.

Mr. Cowley does not say so directly, but I gather he believes, as do I, that no one can claim to be old until their eightieth birthday is behind them. It is obvious to those of us who have lived beyond that magic meridian that the sixties and seventies are merely the infancy and adolescence of maturity. What can a youth of sixty know of being old? If he is an average American man, he is still expecting to make a million and/or be President of the United States. His machismo is galled if matrons with pretty, nubile daughters do not gather them under their skirts when he appears. He is at the peak of his business career and brags about being able to do anything he could accomplish at forty. He is lying a bit about this, but there, growing boys are renowned for exaggeration.

It is not until he passes seventy-five, when "at length the man perceives [the vision] die away, and fade into the light of common day"— my apologies to Wordsworth—that he has any real appreciation of what lies ahead. What *is* there is not all that bad if he has conditioned himself to accept its inevitable handicaps cheerfully. You haven't asked me, but I will tell you anyway, that I think the most important possession for an old person to keep is his brain. The vast bureaucratic establishment interested in gerontology can feed and shelter the aged, but they can't put anything in their heads. Admittedly, something in your stomach is remarkably comforting and will keep you alive, but that is not happiness.

Mr. Cowley uses as an example for his study the members of his class at Harvard, the class of '19. Of the 772 members enrolled, there were at the time he wrote, 208 survivors, almost all octogenarians. He said his general impression was that most were moderately cheerful and moderately active. If sex is important to you, his review suggests you had better number it amongst your memories: Cowley records only one alumnus showing any deep interest in the subject, and he said, "My doctors have forbidden me to chase women unless they are going downhill." (It occurs to me to wonder what he would do if he caught them.) Reading Cowley's recitation of the activities of his classmates suggests that a common thread seems to run through the lives of those who are content, and that is that they are mentally active. None are destitute, of course, and he quotes Cicero's remark that "old age is impossible to bear in extreme poverty, even if one is a philosopher." I do not quarrel with that famous orator's conclusion, but the principal danger here in old age is mental stagnation.

A general opinion held by people who are not old (and mine when I counted myself among them) is that age is a creeping enemy, slowly engulfing its victim like a boa constrictor swallowing a rabbit. The truth is that most whose lives extend beyond eighty remain in quite good health (all things being relative) until the time for departure is near at hand. Cowley points out that those who live to be old are usually those suffering no serious illness during their lifetimes, an opinion held by most students of the subject. They believe that longevity, particularly extreme longevity, is largely genetic in origin. Old age begets old age, and if you have been wise enough to select long-lived ancestors, your chance of emulating them is good. It seems unlikely that avoiding strong drink, jogging three miles a day, or drinking large quantities of the juice that is "not just for breakfast any more" will increase the days of your years. I am strong for the genetic theory because I had a grandmother who lived to be ninety-seven.

I think the thing about old age that annoys me most is finding myself classified. Government studies invariably wind up talking about groups: the old, the blacks, the Hispanics, the veterans, and a dozen other divisions that only the mind of a bureaucrat could devise. They forget that people are people, and any group that can be selected will contain people as different from each other as those outside it. The old have a few characteristics they share in common, but these are of little importance in determining the happiness, intelligence, or ability to adjust to life of the individuals involved.

About the only thing you can say for sure about the old is that they will die sooner than the young, and you can't even say that where individuals are concerned. The only time I am reminded of my age is when I have trouble getting my arms into the sleeves of my overcoat, or when I hang up the long-handled shoehorn I now have to use—and find I have done so on a hook that isn't there. When the conductor does finally blow the whistle heralding my departure, I hope to collapse like a paper bag and get swirled off along the track behind the caboose.

Abigail

A FEW WEEKS ago I wrote a newspaper column about the view from my typewriter. I mentioned a few of the things in sight—which meant also almost within touch, as the room where the typewriter dwells is only about ten feet square, with space taken out by a fireplace, bookshelves, a desk, tables, and chairs. Some people might think it cluttered, and perhaps it is (like my mind), but there is a good deal to be said for clutter. Anyway, I dislike antiseptic surroundings. After you have lived with clutter long enough you have no trouble finding things. The only time you experience difficulty is when, in an excess of housekeeping zeal, the distaff side of the establishment decides the place needs tidying. Then it is a month before anything can again be discovered.

One of the items that puzzles all my visitors is a small, heavy, six-inch-square rosewood frame containing a circlet of braided chestnut hair, with a tiny curl of lighter hair in the center. It has no personal significance. I picked it up in an old junky antique shop many years ago. I really don't know why I bought it, except that it cost but a quarter and I probably thought the frame might come in handy some day. When I got home I dropped it in the bottom drawer of my desk, where it remained undisturbed with other oddments for a long time. Then one day a few years ago I examined it carefully for the first time. The glass was dirty and I couldn't read the faded writing on the yellowed paper on which the hair was mounted, so I took the little rusty tacks out of the back of the frame and spread everything on my desk. The first feeling that came to me, almost as a shock, was a reaction to the quality of the hair. It was smooth and alive and shining, as though it had just been washed and brushed. It was, as I have said, chestnut-colored, but I could now see there were a few little threads of silver running through it. The curl of lighter hair was soft and wound around my finger. The paper backing was stained and brittle, but some writing, though faded, was visible under a magnifying glass. It read:

Mrs. Abigail Y. Perkins,
Died at Lowell, Mass.
October 16th, 1846
Age 36 Yrs.

No reference was made to the little golden curl, which obviously had been snipped from the head of a baby.

I know nothing more of Abigail than this. Today a woman's death in childbirth (or soon thereafer) at age thirty-six, which this pathetic little memorial probably recorded, would be unusual, but in her day it was commonplace. Not only were there fewer hospitals and doctors, and almost all deliveries made at home (where there were no facilities to care for unexpected complications), but women were almost constantly pregnant. There were no contraceptives, as we know them, and except in those cases where women or their husbands were infertile, pregnancy was a frequent condition for married women from the time of their marriage until menopause or death.

Medical science, as we know it today, was nonexistent. There were no anesthetics except alcohol and opium. No one worried too much about the addictive character of the latter, which was prescribed routinely in the form of morphine or laudanum (opium and alcohol—often red wine). Elsie P. Mitchell, writing in a delightful little book called *Our Day*, which is an abridgement of an old family diary, says of the dispensing of opium:

> In nineteenth-century Boston the remedies concocted from the poppy were not considered an addictive snare nor a shameful vice. They were lavishly dispensed for all manner of ailments. Possibly this medical custom was even partly responsible for the peaceful and inspiring deathbed scenes by which the Victorians set such store.

It is difficult for us more fortunate people to translate ourselves into the feelings of our ancestors, to whom early death was a quite normal aspect of life. People loved their children, just as we do, but when it was the norm for a woman to bear a dozen or so children, and then lose half or more of them in infancy or childhood, attitudes were different. Men fell in love then as they do now, but as their wives became pregnant and died with sad regularity, they remarried. It was commonplace for a man to have had three of four wives, and for his family to consist of any number of half-brothers and sisters and vast numbers of cousins of various degrees of consanguinity.

Little Abigail, for whom I have conceived a considerable affection, could have been the second or third wife of Mr. Perkins. She was young by our standards and had years ahead of her. It grieves me that she died as she did. Life for women of that period too closely resembled that of my cows, which calve every year. I think there is something better than that for women, and I am glad that I have lived to see the day when, in America anyway, Abigail's travail can be avoided.

Abigail's *memento mori* hangs on the wall by my study door, where I see it every time I leave the room. Now that the glass has been cleaned, I can distinguish the few silver threads among the brown. I wonder that there are not more.

Superannuated

IF PERADVENTURE, READER, it has been thy lot to waste the golden years of thy life—thy shining youth—in the irksome confinement of an office; to have thy prison days prolonged through middle age down to decrepitude and silver hairs, without hope or release or respite; to have lived to forget there are such things as holidays, or to remember them but as the prerogatives of childhood; then, and then only, will you be able to appreciate my deliverance.

Thus did Charles Lamb begin his famous essay "The Superannuated Man," so I can think of no better introduction to my own few words on retirement.

Since I came to Maine to live, everyone who has visited me, whether intimate friend or complete stranger, has eventually asked my why I did so. Why Maine? Why so far in the country? My answer is that I chose to come here because it was where I thought I would be happiest. That does not satisfy them. They want to know why I expected to be happier here than elsewhere. It is at this point I begin to experience difficulty in supplying plausible reasons—convictions acceptable to them, anyway.

Maine is not a place to which one may retreat to secure what most retirees consider the just rewards of having spent their "shining youth . . . in the irksome confinement of an office." One does not come here because the climate is considerate of old bones; there is usually a foot or so of ice or snow in my dooryard from December until April. There are no shopping centers within walking distance of my home, nor golf courses, horseshoe pitches, Bingo parties, or park benches, where I can while away the tedious hours talking politics with elderly contemporaries. There are no geriatric services waiting to rush to my aid every time my arthritis acts up, nor shining knights with pulmotors and oxygen tanks to succor me if I suffer a heart attack or a cerebral hemorrhage (though we are lucky enough to have a hospital and a volunteer ambulance not too many miles over the horizon). No, the reason I came here is a bit deeper in my subconscious. I think is is because the country, the real country—no exurbia—represents to me a return to the safety and happiness of my childhood.

People who have urban backgrounds complain that there is no privacy in the country, that everyone knows everybody else's business, that you can't even buy anything without a long conversation. This is true, but I enjoy it, and to me the cold impersonal attitude of city life is repelling.

"Aristides," who writes a column for the *American Scholar*, tells a story in that journal that well illustrates the difference in attitude between city and country people. He relates the "all too real . . . joke about the Hoosier who, after two days in New York, asks a native of the city, 'Excuse me, sir, could you tell me where the Empire State Building is, or would you prefer that I go screw myself?'"

Marcus Aurelius, my favorite Roman, said,

> *Men look for retreats, the country, the seashore, the hills . . . yet all this is very unlike a philosopher, when you may at any hour retreat unto yourself. For nowhere does a man retreat into more quiet or more privacy than into his own mind, especially one who has within such things that he has only to look into, and become at once in perfect ease.*

Well, that might have been all right for Marcus Aurelius, but in a city I have great difficulty in retreating into my mind. There is too much hustle and bustle, and too many people hurrying hither and yon intent solely on their own affairs. True, if I ask directions around here I am likely to get a disquisition and an offer to set me on the right road, which will occupy considerable time, but I must admit I consider it preferable to being in the shoes of Aristides' Hoosier.

I do not belittle the value of being able to retreat into one's own mind—I do so frequently—but I find it easier in this ambience. While money is important everywhere, it is less so in the country. The city man has to buy his pleasures, but the country man is more apt to make his own and obtain many of them from contact with his fellows. Urban living places more emphasis on what the world considers to be "progress," which more correctly defined means having more material possessions. There is less of that philosophy in rural areas. People are more apt to consider they are enjoying a satisfactory life if they can maintain a comfortable standard of living pretty much as it has always been. Of course they like to keep up with the times—they prefer flush toilets to outhouses—but there is not that desperate urge afflicting the suburbanite to "keep up with the Joneses." Every man wants safety and comfort for himself and his family, and what he considers necessary to provide that comfort depends upon many things, but in the country it is not so likely to mean having more, ever more, of what he already has.

These are some of the reasons why, on the way to decrepitude and silver hair, I have chosen to live in the country.

Church

WHEN I WAS filing out of church with my fellow sinners a couple of weeks ago, a friend stopped me and said, "Roy, I have something amusing for you. A reader of your essays asked me if you really did go to church." "What did you reply?" I questioned. "Oh, I just told him that of course you did, and that you even preached a sermon once in a while."

The question suggests that the picture developed by my essays does not coincide with the popular notion of how a churchgoer is supposed to think and behave. Maybe it doesn't. I have never considered my essays as revealing my religious inclinations, and had I been asked would have said they merely portray an average, reasonably literate countryman going about his daily duties, attending church being one of them.

The truth is that churches accommodate all kinds of people. Non-churchgoers seem to think of the mental processes of those who attend church with some regularity as being uniform and a good deal more devoted to religion than they really are. We who attend church are, after all, just like everybody else. We have livings to make, probably spouses and kids to think about, and we spend most of our time worrying about all the thousand-and-one things that impinge upon everyone's life between one day and the next.

I said once that I went to church for the same reason I drink champagne (when I can afford it)—to give me a lift. Although they might not express themselves in those same words, I am convinced others do the same. Few people go around all week thinking about God, and a good many don't stretch their minds in that direction to any great extent even on Sundays. What happens is that by attending church one finds oneself in the company of others who are also looking for a lift, and who, pretty generally, admit they could make a better job of their lives if they took time once a week to think about it.

I have been going to church since I was about six years old—anyway, that is as far back as I can remember doing so. It is a habit. The inside of a church is as familiar to me as the inside of any of the several houses I have lived in. It is not a holy temple where I come to pray but a place where I can be with my friends and listen to a preacher who may possibly (no guarantee) drop a thought into my mind that will, like a stone dropped into a still pool, continue to make circles long after it has reached the bottom.

The ritual of religion is important to some people and of no moment to others. Churchgoers not infrequently make quite a pother about things that have no bearing upon man's virtue. They disagree about whether one should use "debts" or "trespasses" in the Lord's

Prayer. (When this arises I am always reminded of the famous gardener Gertrude Jekyll, who hated the commercialization of Christmas, and prayed, "Forgive us our Christmasing as we forgive those who Christmas against us.")

I remember once, when I was a little boy, asking my grandmother what people did when they bowed their heads for a few moments after they entered their pew. As best I can recall, she was a little flustered and answered that they said the Lord's Prayer. Maybe they do—or perhaps it's some private orison—but I have a pretty good idea that what is going on in a number of those reverently bowed heads is a wondering whether they turned off the gas under the teakettle or let the dog out for a mini-run before they closed him in for a couple of hours.

The importance of ritual depends to some extent on your church. You have, for instance, the Church of Rome and the Society of Friends—about as far apart as you can get. I have attended both and can assure those who are interested that while there are differences in formula, there is little difference in people. Currently I attend a Congregational church that accommodates all shades of thought. We run the gamut from born-again Christians to Emersonian Unitarians. I guess I belong among the latter.

We recently had a small hassle about what kind of a man we should ask to be our new minister, the old one having retired. The Evangelicals leaned one way and people like myself, another. Among the "born-agains" was a young lady who claimed sudden conversion while lying on the hot sands of an island in the West Indies. As I have an abiding suspicion of Saul-on-the-road-to-Damascus conversions, it is not difficult to understand that we were on opposite sides. However—and this is what is important—we are both interested in the same objective. She wants to build a steeple to the glory of God, while my more earthly ambition is to construct something that will help man *ad astra per aspera*, without worrying too much about theological gobbledygook. The funny thing is that when we climbed the last scaffold to place our respective crosses on the steeple, we found each other face-to-face.

The Gallery

LIKE MOST PEOPLE who live in our village, we eat our meals in the kitchen. If there are only a couple of guests we feed them there too, but if there are more, we go for broke and use the dining room. Our kitchen table, which seats four with the leaf up, faces the road and, beyond it, the bay. I say "faces the road," and it does, but there is a closed porch (which we call the "gallery" when we are being grandiloquent) that we look across.

The gallery has evolved on its own—like Topsy, it "jest grow'd." When we bought the place there was no porch, so we added one, for what sort of a Maine house would it be with a view of the water but no "piazza" to sit on? If you don't know it, though, open porches facing the water hereabouts are pretty draughty. There may be a few days in the summer when you can enjoy them, but ten months of the year you have to settle for their architectural enhancement of your property, and ask no more.

Our weather being what it is, it was not long before we decided that by not going to Florida for the winter we could afford to close in the porch and enjoy Florida in Maine. (Of course we avoided the detail that we have never been to Florida for the winter anyway—because that would have eliminated our excuse for spending the money (plenty of it, for six pieces of 6-foot by 12-foot Thermopane). Having thus adroitly saved enough money to do the job and salved our economic consciences, we went ahead. We have never regretted it.

Our house, which was built in 1852 and largely rebuilt by us in 1958, faces east. It had to be rebuilt to be sure it wouldn't collapse around our ears, but even so it looks much the same externally, barring a few bits we chopped off and gave away; and it *is* on the original foundation. Our gallery, then, faces east also. It is ten feet wide and forty feet long, with the entrance door at the south end. The gallery is thus ideally situated both to grow plants and to act as a buffer, protecting the kitchen and dining room and parlor against the easterlies that tear unhindered across the bay. East and south are the perfect exposures for a conservatory, which is what the gallery really is. The morning light floods in the moment the sun slips above the horizon, and in the winter when the sun remains low, sunlight brightens the gallery the whole day. In the summer, when we can do without so much sun, it is high overhead by noon, while the inside of the gallery remains in grateful shade.

I think midwinter is when I enjoy the gallery most. I am often asked if heating is not expensive. It is not. We installed a minimum of electric heat, just enough to keep the temperature at about forty-five degrees on a winter night. Not much is needed because one side of the gallery is a house wall. In the day, the sun keeps it warm regardless of outside temperature. Frequently, even with the temperature at zero outside, we have to open the transom to keep the place from getting too hot. The gallery is also blessed with a sort of microclimate because its solid roof makes shade along the house wall. It is there that we grow ferns (staghorn) and ivies, and such begonias and epiphyllums as require shade. The glory of the winter, though, is in the camellias.

Twenty or more years ago Helen and I made a trip to Charleston, South Carolina, to see the Magnolia Gardens and Middleton Place in connection with an article I was writing. It was at camellia time, and we were entranced by their beauty. I remember that, at Middleton Place particularly, the camellia bushes were trees, reaching high over our heads. On our way home we passed a small nursery with balled and burlapped camellia plants standing by the side of the road. I couldn't resist the temptation, and although I had no idea where I was going to put it, stopped and bought a plant labeled R.L. Wheeler. Ever since, that camellia has unfailingly presented us with five-inch, luscious pink flowers, and now it is six feet tall, although I must have pruned away a foot each year for that score of years. For the first year or so I kept it in the greenhouse in increasingly larger pots, but finally, once the gallery was complete, I had somewhere to put it. I made a cypress tub sixteen inches wide and high, in which the camellia has flourished ever since.

Camellias are wonderful plants. They need a minimum of attention, and reward the gardener without stint. In summer they must have shade, which we give them by placing them under a lath house or a tree, and in the winter they need sunshine but a cool temperature. A night temperature of forty-five to fifty degrees is best. Perfect drainage and constant moisture are the other requirements, with some fertilizer, preferably acid, at the time they are making new growth.

The Spider

As I LAY ON my bed this morning after sunup, I observed a speck overhead, like a grain of black sand on the vast white Sahara of my bedroom ceiling. By and by it seemed to move, though it was so small, and its resting place so without point of reference, that had it not been an old familiar I would not have been certain. It was, perhaps, a millimeter across, about as large as the head of a pin—a small pin. If I took my eyes off it for a moment, it seemed to vanish and I had to hunt for it again. But, as I said, it was an old acquaintance and has been performing its inverted trapeze act for me for months. Of course, it may be a different spider from the one I first saw; I am not so familiar with the differences in the tribe that I can take an oath on it, and except on one occasion when it obligingly sat still on a window casing and allowed me to examine it with a magnifying glass, I have never had a close look. After all, about six feet separates my pillow from the ceiling, and even keen sight (which I no longer possess) does not magnify a millimeter into anything vast at that distance.

About fifteen minutes after I first saw my friend this morning, he/she had progressed by short rushes to a point directly over my head. (I am not very knowledgeable about the sex of spiders either, except that I read the lady eats the gentleman—literally, not figuratively—after copulation, and that if he is not fast enough off the mark she will even eat him before he has his fun.) As though it had reached a predetermined destination, the spider let itself down on a silken strand to a point in space about six inches above my nose. It considered me for a few moments, swaying from side to side as I breathed, and then suddenly climbed back up to the ceiling. I wondered what it did with its trapeze, for when it had accomplished its climb, nothing was to be seen.

Most people do not know that my friend and neighbor, E.B. White, in addition to being a fine essayist and the author of *Charlotte's Web*, wrote some beautiful poetry. I was reminded of a few lines of his:

THE SPIDER DROPPING DOWN FROM TWIG,

UNWINDS A THREAD OF HER DEVISING;

A THIN, PREMEDITATED RIG

TO USE IN RISING.

The thing that most interests me, and has given me wonder for many years, is that here in this tiny speck is finished creation, sentient life. That it traps and consumes food is not so remarkable, for that is sparked by hunger, which is a completely physical condition, but that it also experiences fear and retreats from my inquiring finger (a mental, not physical response) is remarkable.

When I was a little boy I used to look at our big family Bible, which had pictures of the Ark and Noah herding lions and tigers and elephants up a precarious-looking gangplank, and I supposed that there were also smaller creatures. I asked Grandma about all the "creepy-crawly things"–did they go aboard too? She answered that of course they did, and pointed out that the Bible says, "There went in two and two . . . male and female." I didn't know in those days that there are forty thousand species of spiders alone, and goodness knows how many other creepy-crawlies. Lesser statistics were impressive enough. I wondered where Noah put them all. I didn't know either that this was one of the fairy-story parts of the Bible, but it still gives me wonder today, now I am a big boy, that such myriad forms of life have developed on earth, which itself is to the whole universe as that tiny speck of spider on my bedroom ceiling is to the Milky Way galaxy, which I can see from the road in front of Amen Farm on any cold, clear winter night.

Friends and Neighbors

WE HAD OUR first pullet egg this morning. I hope it means the old birds, which have been in a moult for the last two months, will also begin to produce again. Enough time has passed since they went off lay for them to have gotten their act together. It seems to me that we either have our refrigerator half-full of eggs or I can't find even one for breakfast. Most of the time there are too many. Just for our own use,

A Countryman's Farewell
130

we could probably get along with the production of two birds, but who ever heard of having a flock of two hens? I could, of course, give up keeping them altogether and buy my eggs at the store, but the "fresh eggs" *they* sell are from ten to thirty days old, and if you are accustomed to catching your egg as it drops from the hen, you notice the difference.

Anyway, I have given up almost everything else around here. No cattle, which once used to greet me in the barn with a "flop" and a rattle of their stanchion chains and a reaching for the wisp of hay or greenery I always gave them so they would look for me; no more sheep playing "I'm the king of the castle" on the pasture boulders on moonlit nights; no more pigs that I could never look at without thinking of that frill, or curtain, of pure white fat separating a pig's abdomen from its chest cavity. (Forgive me, you tenderhearted ones who have never seen your lard on the hoof.) No more turkeys. I miss the turkeys most; they are such stately, slow-moving birds. They speak in a fluid little whistle, approach in their dignified manner, cock their heads to one side, and then, like lightning, remove from your sleeve—or your fingernail, for that matter—some tiny fragment you can barely see. They do it precisely, too; you cannot feel them touch you (a fact you'll never find mentioned in a poultry book).

The wildlings are still with us, although not so many swallows since the cattle are gone. The swallows fed on the flies and other insects that inhabited the pile of barn dressing. Chicken manure does not seem to work quite the same way. The rest of the freeloaders are still around, though, and now that I have lived here a third of a lifetime I know where to find them. Not on order, perhaps, but often enough to confirm my knowledge of the places they frequent.

There is a particular boulder in my back hayfield that foxes use pretty regularly to survey their domain. They are alert to any movement, looking, I suppose, for the "mice and rats and such small deer" that had been "Tom's food for seven long year." I never see a fox in that spot but I am reminded of the endpapers of a book called *Men of Concord*. It is, of course, a collection of writings by Henry David Thoreau, illustrated by N.C. Wyeth. I value it particularly because Wyeth autographed my copy for me. The painting is of Thoreau, downhill across a couple of snow-covered fields, with a fox in the foreground.

I see bears regularly, usually in the spring. They are not around now, of course; they have better sense and are denned up somewhere for the winter. I have never seen one after November, but I am told a warm spell may bring them out for a day or so. I did see one late last October. I was driving home from the village and looked up a dirt lane opening onto the Naskeag road. It wasn't a very big bear—this year's cub, I'd say. It was standing on all fours in the middle of the lane, looking sort of lonely. I don't know what happened to it, because I went by the end of the lane too fast, but if I could have given it any advice, it would have been to stay the hell off the roads. If it is seen, somebody will shoot it, season or no season. Bears are really quite inoffensive characters, even if they do steal your garbage—but so do coons and skunks, of which we have a-plenty.

When I went down-cellar the other day to get some apples, I found the mice had sampled a couple of them and also had made a start on seven enormous Comice pears a friend had sent us. I protected the apples by hoisting the basket well off the ground with a piece of binder-twine, and took the pears upstairs and ate them. (That was no problem.) Today I saw the culprit. He was scurrying, in that flickering way mice have, among some oranges and grapefruit we had been sent from Florida, but he hadn't bothered them. I guess mice "and other small deer" get along without "Florida Sunshine."

As for the large deer, they are still around in spite of all the local Robin Hoods. I saw two sets of tracks in the snow this morning. One looked big enough for a moose, but as moose only wander down here in the spring, I exculpate that tribe. It must have been a doe, and the little prints those of a fawn.

Ivar told me that the mouse I saw was the one I had refused to kill a couple of weeks ago and had set loose in the garden. *Quien sabe?* Mice have to eat, too.

Anglo-American English

HAVING BEEN BORN an American but educated in England, I have all my life had trouble deciding whether to write English English or the American version. When I say I have had trouble, it would suggest that every time I write something I make a conscious decision; of course I do not. Nobody writes in that fashion, so I have trained myself out of writing "kerb" instead of "curb," when I am writing about a sidewalk (which in England is called a "pavement"), but I must remember that the English "curb" a horse just as we do, and that "kerb" is limited to a kerbstone. I am also able to remember that when a lady in England is "knocked-up" she is tired and exhausted, not pregnant. Also, when I am in England, I usually remember that "bloody" is an expletive and rarely means covered with blood, so that a "bloody fool" doesn't mean quite the same thing it does on this side of the Atlantic.

There are also everyday items of communication that are not bilingual. When in America, I remember to ask for "lamb chops" and not "lamb cutlets," and I don't go into a restaurant and demand a couple of "rashers" of bacon with my fried egg. "Biscuits" in England are the thin, hard things we call crackers here, not light objects like blueberry muffins without the blueberries. I don't believe I have ever seen a biscuit (American) in England, the nearest thing being a scone— which is a very delectable object in its own right, particularly when it is an ingredient of Thunder and Lightning (a scone liberally slathered with strawberry jam and Devonshire cream).

On a more earthy level, a "flush" as we call it in Maine (or more generally in the nation, a "john") becomes a "WC" or a "loo" in England. I have never heard the work "crapper" used over there; in America it has a slightly indelicate connotation, but nevertheless it is purported to be the cognomen of the gentleman who invented the flush toilet.

In this country it is hard to avoid, either in restaurants or supermarkets, the "English muffin." In England I have never seen an English muffin, certainly not in the last thirty years. I think I did in my youth, but that is so long ago that I can't be sure I really saw one, or only knew about them through a nursery rhyme about the muffin man. I have bought crumpets in an American supermarket and can recommend them, but I don't recall seeing them in England since my childhood, when crumpets, along with fresh bread, used to be delivered in a baker's cart.

I have learned to spell words like "harbor" and "labor" and "honor" without the u, but I still think that "honorable" is more honorable when the u is included. Such words as "when" and "where" and "what" are usually aspirated initially by the educated English, coming out as "hwen," "hware," and "hwot," whereas most Americans just say "wen," "wear," and "wot." There is, of course, no right or wrong, merely a difference, although I must say the aspirated pronunciation has a more pleasant sound. On the other hand, my English friends tease me about saying "got" and "gotten," words that have fallen into disuse in their country except when used with a prefix, like "ill-gotten."

On the whole, I think the English are more precise in their use of the language. For instance, one does not so frequently hear the word "like" used in such barbarisms as "like I said" instead of "as I said." I forget now who made the observation, but a professor (American) of English literature once remarked that soon he expected to hear his students saying "Like You Like It," for Shakespeare's *As You Like It*. Other illustrations that could be cited involve the words "further" and "farther," which are almost interchangeable in America. In England, "further" indicates "in addition to," and "farther" means "more distant or remote."

The word "lend" seems to be less common in the American vocabulary, where "loan" is used instead. Fowler says: "Loan. The verb has been expelled from idiomatic southern English by Lend, but was formerly current, and survives in U.S. and locally in U.K." Having been brought up to believe that I could "lend" something to someone, but accept a "loan" if they were lending something to me, it is difficult for me not to get linguistic goose-bumps when someone asks me to loan them something.

I think, perhaps, that the everyday Englishman has more fun with his language than do we. Even among the less well-educated, you will hear specifics instead of generalities. This is particularly true in the country, where collectives that we never hear are used to designate groups of animals. We use some too, of course, such as a bed of clams or a shoal of fish or a pack of hounds, but the English countryman talks of a brace of pheasants or ducks (meaning two, usually dead), a charm of goldfinches, a cry of hounds, a drove of cattle or sheep, an exaltation of larks (which is a definition utterly delightful), a flight of birds (they also designate lakes where water birds congregate as flight ponds), a skein or a gaggle of geese, and so forth.

I think that country people generally, regardless of nationality, are more specific. A city person is likely to call anything bovine a cow, whereas the countryman will refer to a bull or a heifer or a calf or a first calf heifer or a steer or a yearling bull. When referring to sheep, he will talk of a ewe or a ram or a cosset lamb or a tup—whereas to the urbanite they are all sheep.

It is sad that so many young people in America today speak and write only basic English; and this is not limited to those not having had the advantages of a higher education. Certainly it is possible to communicate with a vocabulary of a few hundred words, but he who does so is a linguistic paraplegic. The blame for this, or a large part of it, can be laid to the fact that most children spend an enormous amount of time listening to television, where, except for a few programs, the scripts are so verbally limited. Children cannot learn to speak or write precise and interesting English, or express themselves in any but the most general terms, unless they read extensively—and read books by authors who have the ability to write with color, clarity, and exactness. I can remember being told by my schoolmaster that if he heard me use "nice" improperly even once during the coming week, he would cane me. I did, and he did. He pointed out that the word nice meant precise and exact, not that Aunt Susie was a pleasant lady or that the food was tasty or that it was a warm and sunny day.

It is difficult to apportion blame for this unhappy state of affairs. Certainly much of it belongs at home, where children listen to linguistically crippled parents, but educators cannot be held blameless. When I was at school I learned English, not only in my English classes but from all other teachers, who corrected my grammar even if their official subject was, let us say, geography. Nowadays, on television or in social conversation, I listen to teachers who make me wince. They are, perhaps, excellent science teachers, but it would not subtract from their ability if they were also able to speak English—either the American or English variety.

Love

I was listening a few nights ago to Felice Leonardo Buscaglia, who lectures on love. He does a very good job of it. That it is a subject close to all our hearts was evidenced by the response of the audience. He got off to a slow start. His listeners sat on their hands, and I thought to myself, Well, he is not going to have much success with these frigid New Englanders. But I was wrong. It just took him a little longer to thaw them out, but he did—and by the time he had mopped his brow for the last time, there was a pretty girl rushing from her seat to hug him, just as happens west of the Rockies. A desire for love, for affection, is universal and close to the surface in all of us, but we are so inhibited by the mores of our society that we fear to show it. Or we are embarrassed, which is much the same thing.

Although I am not a professional preacher, just a pinch-hitter, I would like to preach a sermon on love. I am not much for Biblical texts—when I hear a preacher support everything he says with a verse from the Bible, I back into my shell and close the lid—but there is a good text if you want to talk of love, in Corinthians 1:13, to the effect that no matter what virtues you practice, you'll miss by a country mile if you do so without love. You may give to the United Way or support Alcoholics Anonymous, but unless you do it with real personal involvement and affection, all you are trying to do is to buy your way into heaven or salve your conscience.

I said one day that I didn't think much of faith the way it is understood by church people. Their use of it makes me think of H.L. Mencken's observation that "faith may be defined briefly as an illogical belief in the occurrence of the improbable." Love, though—even if you can't see, taste, smell, or touch it—is obvious. But I agree with Leo Buscaglia that a hug is a help. I don't know why we North Americans, New Englanders particularly, are so afraid of physical contact. Perhaps it is because with our Puritan heritage we think of love and sex as being different words for the same thing. We are afraid if we touch another man we are on our way toward being a homosexual, and if it is a woman, that we have designs on her person.

A need for affection is part of our makeup. The first thing to happen to us when we are born, is to be taken in our mother's arms—and it is a long time before we leave them. If a person shrinks from physical contact, and a few do, I am sorry for them, for I know they were deprived in their childhood, and they will never be able to enjoy life to its fullest.

Some few people who pass across this world's stage play such great parts they are never forgotten, but most of us are only stagehands or electricians and are never seen by the audience. For us there can never be any blast of trumpets or great impersonations to be remembered by, but, in our obscurity, there is a role for us: we can be remembered for our kindness and our loving regard for others. To play the part, we do not need a script or prompter in the wings (though the latter might not be a bad idea), and if the recollection of us lasts no longer than the memories of those who were our fellows, it can still be a loving one.

I think the only usefulness a preacher has is to express love. The moment he is seen as a pragmatist or a technician he might as well get into some other profession. There is no more virtue in being able to repeat the Athanasian Creed (or any other formula for that matter)—and it does no more good—than being able to repeat Mary Poppins's "supercaliphragilisticexpealidocious." I can still repeat the Greek alphabet from alpha to omega, but what I got out of my school days that was useful was not a smidgeon of ancient Greek but a knowledge of the amazing diversity of human beings and an understanding that the common need for all of us is affection. I learned also what Leo Buscaglia reminded me, that we don't kick dogs with wagging tails. Maybe that memory might help prevent wars.

I'd like to close this short homily with a quotation, the words of an anonymous poet are inscribed on a sundial at the University of Virginia, in Charlottesville:

TIME

IS

TOO SLOW FOR THOSE WHO WAIT

TOO SWIFT FOR THOSE WHO FEAR,

TOO LONG FOR THOSE WHO GRIEVE,

TOO SHORT FOR THOSE WHO REJOICE,

BUT FOR THOSE WHO LOVE, TIME IS

ETERNITY.

HOURS FLY,

FLOWERS DIE,

NEW DAYS,

NEW WAYS,

PASS BY.

LOVE STAYS.

Winter

137

Crows

THERE IS NOTHING more evocative of loneliness than the sight of a crow beating heavily into a raw east wind over a bleak winter landscape. Not a landscape whitened by snow, for that gives light and shadow, but a sunless scene of uniform darkness, where the naked, leafless trees can barely be distinguished against the background of dull winter evergreens. The bird moves as though swimming rather than flying. Its wing beats are slow and laborious and seem just enough to keep it afloat, but it continues on until the sight of it is lost over the lifeless waters of the bay.

I cannot say I have an affection for crows, but when, as now, there are no other birds to be seen, not even a gull, or a blue jay (to whom the crow is related), I accept them. I fill the bird feeders hoping for the sight of chickadees, evening grosbeaks, goldfinches, all those dozen or so species that partake of my bounty during the winter, and all I get are crows. There are three perched in the topmost branches of an apple tree, waiting for me to hang out the suet sticks, which they will empty before any other bird can get to them. I tell myself I hate them and that I will shoot them, as that is the only way to be rid of their presence. But of course I won't. I am not like the English country gentleman who is alleged to have said, "What a beautiful day. Let's go out and kill something." I did shoot a crow once, about fifteen years ago, and I have never done so since. It flopped around for a few minutes before it died, and I thought it said, with Poe's raven, "Nevermore," and that is the way it has been. I am not a very successful killer. In my youth I shot a few pheasants and partridges (but in exculpation I plead that I ate them for supper), and I confess to slaughtering farm animals for food. Even in those cases, though, I felt queasy. I guess I am one of those cowards who would rather pay a professional in Chicago or Kansas City to do my killing for me where I don't have to watch it being done.

If you want to know about crows, you should refer to the second volume of Forbush's *Birds of Massachusetts*, where ten pages are devoted to their description and habits, together with dozens of anecdotes about them. You will soon come to the conclusion that they are exceedingly intelligent birds and, like humans, completely omnivorous. If there is anything a crow will not eat, I have yet to learn of it; and the same may, be said of *Homo sapiens*, who consumes anything from dead pigs to live oysters to seaweed. Ivar told me that he had caught two mice in the cellar yesterday. He put their corpses on the stone wall near the bird feeder, and in a twinkling they were gone. Forbush says that "the stomach of a young Crow seems to approximate that of a bottomless pit. They require to be fed almost constantly. Two of my assistants once kept some young Crows in confinement which required at least half their own weight of food daily, and would eat even more if they could get it."

Crows are both migrants and common residents. They leave the colder part of the state in the winter and spend it on the coast, where they can forage along the shore. I have watched them walking—stalking would be a better word—along the littoral, peering into crevices and dropping mussels onto the rocks to break them, as do the gulls. Fish to fruit, it is all one to them. Ivar told me this morning when I spoke to him about raking up the fallen apples littering the ground under a couple of large wild apple trees, "There aren't any. The crows cleaned up the whole lot."

When I was a small boy it was commonplace for crows to be kept as pets. If caged or otherwise imprisoned when young, they soon become part of the family, and as long as they are fed, they will hang around. They can be taught to talk like a parrot, and entertain by a dozen mischievous tricks. They are inveterate thieves and, like tamed starlings, collect bright trinkets. Ornithologically our crows are *Corvus brachyrhynchos*, if that is of any interest to you. The raven, of which we have a few, is *Corvus corax principalis*, and the English rook, a relative, is *Corvus frugiligus*. Rooks nest in colonies in the tops of trees. There seem to be hundreds of them. Once a year in the summer, after the young are fledged and flying, a sport of the English (if that is what you can call it) is to gather together a group of people with twenty-gauge guns for an afternoon of rook-shooting. I don't remember what they do with the victims; maybe they are the ingredients for "Four and twenty blackbirds baked in a pie."

Reincarnation

IF I AM EVER reincarnated in the flesh (which I think unlikely) and have any choice as to the identity in which I am to be clothed, I should like it to be as a priest. If this startles you, read on, and I will reveal my reasons.

If I am granted my preference, I should like to return as an Anglo-Catholic priest, Anglo-Catholic simply because I want my wife to share my reincarnation. I do not believe, even in the spiritual body of reincarnation, I would be a good candidate for chastity. On the other hand, if Rome goes the way of all flesh, as it periodically shows signs of doing, then I would be as happy in one branch of Catholicism as another. I do not believe I could accept reincarnation as a noncon-formist minister, because with a few exceptions the Protestant church has spent its efforts ever since the Reformation inveighing against the world, the flesh, and the Devil. Although I have never met him, the Devil is described on good ecclesiastical authority as a very unpleasant fellow. On the other hand, I am happy to admit I have a great affection for the world and the flesh—after all, if I had not, I would not want to be reincarnated.

The foregoing may seem strange coming from a long-time Con-gregationalist, but I have observed in my fairly extensive reading over the last eighty years or so that Catholics (of whatever persuasion) seem to have the most fun, and are interested in those things that appeal to me. Uniformly, they show in their writings, particularly in their diaries, that they are first-rate gardeners. Dean S. Reynolds Hole (who wrote about having beautiful roses in one's heart) was the first great modern rosarian. Then there was Henry Nicholson Ellacombe, Honor-able Canon of Bristol, Vicar of Bitton and Rural Dean, who was re-puted to have a greater variety of plants in his garden, and to have received and given away more rare plants, than anyone else then living. (He lived to be ninety-four, which shows what a garden will do for you.) Father Cupani, who described the sweet pea (a Sicilian wild flower) in his *Hortus Catholicus* as long ago as 1697, sent seeds to Doctor Robert Uvedale in England, whence they ultimately migrated to California, where sweet-pea seed is now grown by the ton. There are dozens, perhaps hundreds, of other notable priestly gardeners—a description of whose quiet and gentle avocation would fill several books—but there is no room for them here. However, I cannot close without just mentioning the names of Père Armand David, a French missionary in China, who introduced, in addition to many other plants, what is probably the most beautiful flowering tree in the world—the Davidia; and the Reverend Gilbert White, who has been called the father of field ornithology, but who also was a notable gardener and diarist.

I suppose it was because they were so wrapped up in the evangelical view of religion that nonconformist ministers had little time for the gentler and more enjoyable aspects of life. People like John Wesley for instance (who was barely a nonconformist and would have been horrified by the later aspects of Methodism) kept diaries so steeped in the conviction of personal guilt that they are barely readable today. On the other hand, our knowledge of the daily life of the eighteenth and nineteenth centuries (other than as relating to politics and wars) would be barren were it not for the records of Anglo-Catholics like the Reverend Francis Kilvert, Parson Woodforde, and the Reverend William Cole, to mention just three. Their daily contacts with their parishioners, the way they traveled, what they wore and read, and—most of all—what they ate, open a window on their times. Woodforde, living deep in the East Anglian countryside, where the population was about as scanty as it is in Maine, tells in great detail of the parties he attended, the meals he ate (which were stupendous, but which he shared with all his poor neighbors), and all the many joys and sorrows of country living.

It has always seemed to me that a parson of whatever cut of cloth should illustrate for his flock not only the theological and spiritual aspects of Christianity, but the more intellectual, comfortable, loving, and gentler sides of life. He should enjoy a good meal (and know how to cook it, and perhaps be able to mix a good dry martini). He should enjoy and use wine in moderation and should admire lovely ladies. I insist that he be well-read and cultured and know something besides where to find in the Bible a verse to nail down everything he says, like a cobbler with a mouthful of tacks. In brief, he should be able to show by example that the world is here to be lived in and enjoyed and that religion is not just a penance to be suffered until you wind up either in heaven or hell. I think in recent years nonconformist ministers, or maybe just a modest number of them, are coming around to this philosophy. In the past it has not been true, which is why I want to be reincarnated as an Anglo-Catholic.

This subject came to me last night, when I was in bed reading the latest book by Father Robert Farrar Capon. He is, currently, my favorite priest. I have known him some time, ever since he published a book called *The Supper of the Lamb*, which I bought because I liked the title. I looked at it briefly, paid my $5.95, took it home, and thought, I would like to belong to that man's church. (No reflection upon my present minister, with whom I am well pleased.) If you don't know Father Capon—a wonderful name for a cook, by the way—I urge you to buy *The Supper of the Lamb* and make his acquaintance. He is married and has six children, and he enjoys living. He says of women, "They are like cheese strudels. When first baked, they are crisp and fresh outside, but the filling is unsettled and indigestible; in age, the crust may not be so lovely but the filling comes at last into its own."

McClure's

ALTHOUGH, AS I HAVE written before, I am a dedicated snapper-up of unconsidered trifles, my greatest enthusiasm comes to the fore when I am exposed to the temptations offered by a secondhand bookstore. Although the books I already own fill my house from ground floor to attic—crowding the hallways, kitchen, and bedrooms, with the overflow going to a guest cottage where we isolate visitors—I still cannot resist buying more.

Like most book-lovers, I have several areas of interest, and something is always coming along that fits into one collection or another like a piece in a jigsaw puzzle. When I received a note from a bookseller who sends me lists of diaries that come his way, I remembered that I own several hundred already, but there is, of course, no end to diaries. No one could find all that have been written, not even just those that have been printed, let alone those in manuscript, but every time I am told of one I do not own, I can no more avoid buying it than a child can resist a candy bar or a young man a pretty girl. (The note I refer to was from New Englandiana, P.O. Box 589, Bennington, Vermont 05201. I give the detail as a service to other book lovers, as New Englandiana's lists are diversified and the books listed are interesting and inexpensive.)

But I am getting off the track. What I intended to write about is an old magazine given me by a friend. If you are known as a bibliophile you don't have to buy all your books and magazines—your kind friends remember your weakness. There are not many worthwhile magazines nowadays (television has killed them the way airplanes sank the great ocean liners), but not so long ago there were many, and they boasted large circulations and employed the talents of outstanding writers and artists of the day. Names like *Munsey*, *Cosmopolitan*, *The Atlantic*, *Harper's*, and *McClure's* were to be found on every newsstand. Most are gone, so I was interested when my friend gave me a copy of the *McClure's* Christmas issue from 1895, when the magazine was in its heyday. *McClure's* was not a cheap publication filled with stories of ephemeral interest, to be thrown out with the trash as soon as it had been read; it was a volume of some 150 pages beautifully printed on good paper, carrying numerous fine black-and-white illustrations. Many subscribers to magazines of this class had them bound for permanent possession. They had ongoing literary value. Furthermore, they cost less than a newspaper does today: *McClure's* was only ten cents a copy, or one dollar by the year.

My copy of *McClure's* opens with a story of Abraham Lincoln edited by Ida M. Tarbell, and it contains by far the best picture of Lincoln I have ever seen. This was from an ambrotype taken by C. Jackson in Pittsfield, Illinois, in 1855. In addition to the Lincoln piece, which is an installment of a long study, there is a short story by Anthony Hope (author of *The Prisoner of Zenda*), an article by Will Low on the "Madonna and Child in Art" with more than thirty illustrations (remember this was a Christmas number), an article about her family by Elizabeth Stuart Phelps, stories by Hall Caine and several others, and an interesting historical piece about Annie Laurie. For future issues the editor promised such writers as Bret Harte, Robert Louis Stevenson, Ian MacLaren, and Rudyard Kipling, plus portraits of Henry Wadsworth Longfellow and Mark Twain. Indeed, a goodly company.

Even though this issue of the magazine was published only a little while before I was born, its advertisements seem to be from a much earlier era. It is amazing, though, how many of the firms we know in 1988 were going strong in 1895. On the back cover, Ivory Soap already has started to float along for the Procter and Gamble Company, and next to their quarter-page ad, the Baker Chocolate people (established in 1780) complain that their success has "led to the placing on the market many misleading and unscrupulous imitations." Elsewhere, Sapolio, Quaker Oats, Ed. Pinaud, Cabot's Creosote Shingle Stain, and the Eastman Kodak Company remind you of their products. From Eastman you could buy a Pocket Kodak for five dollars, and a developing and printing outfit for a dollar-fifty. (I can well remember home-developing, when you hid in the hall closet with a small red-globed kerosene lamp, hoping your "snaps" would not all be light-struck.) On an inside page was a fascinating picture of a "Faultless Quaker Dishwasher" (hand-operated) with a handle on top, so the busy housewife could spin the dishes without getting her hands in the water. Best of all, though, was the men's "Hub Combination Suit," including extra trousers and a matching cap, warranted all wool, offered by Jordan, Marsh and Company for five dollars! (Samples of cloth sent free by mail.)

Maybe our grandfathers did not collect as many pieces of green paper at the end of a week as we do, but they could change what they had into silver (or gold, if they had as much as ten dollars), and they paid no income tax and not many other taxes. They could get a year's reading for a dollar, a suit and extra pants for five dollars, and some Dr. Hobbs "Sparagus" kidney pills that would cure them of "all kidney diseases . . . all blood troubles of which kidney disorders are the beginning . . . rheumatism, gout, neuralgia, anemia, headache, sleeplessness, backache etc." for fifty cents. They could also buy a Champion typewriter for fifteen dollars, which should have appealed to many aspiring young writers.

Caring

I WAS SITTING at my typewriter this morning when Nancy came in and asked if I knew where the binoculars were. I replied they were on the chest in my bedroom where I often keep them so I can look down the bay and see what is happening. (I look out to sea the way landlocked people look down the street.) Was there any particular reason, I asked, why she needed them? Her reply got me on my feet at once. She said that Freddy Allen's craft had capsized and all the other fishermen in the area were trying to get him out of the water and save his boat.

I doubt many people, except those who live on the coast, think much about any danger being attached to providing the scallops they eat, but actually there is never a season passes that does not see some fatality or near-fatality among the fishermen. Scalloping involves dragging a heavy chain net across the bottom of the bay and hoisting it up at intervals to pick out the scallops and discard all the other cultch that comes up with them. Although offshore scalloping is a year-round occupation, here on the coast it is limited to the winter months. Lobstering takes priority all summer, but come November the lobstermen haul their traps and scalloping takes over. Our winter weather is not balmy, and sea water on the Maine coast is never what one would call tepid. In the winter it hovers around forty degrees Fahrenheit and is colder on the surface just before the ice makes. You don't have to remain in it very long before your vital signs vanish.

We had one fatality already this winter: a boat with a crew of three capsized in Jericho Bay, off Swans Island. Two men were saved, but the captain was lost. I am not sure what happened, but some part of the gear carried away and the boat was flipped over. Most accidents are associated with the drag fouling or some part of the gear breaking. Most inshore scallopers work from the same boats they use for lobstering during the summer, and a heavy drag is not the easiest thing to handle in a smallish boat. With lobstermen, the commonest cause of death is due to a man getting his foot or leg caught in a trap warp and being hauled overboard with the trap. There is not much he can do; it is like being thrown overboard with an anchor hung on your feet.

When I went upstairs with the binoculars I could see several boats gammed up on the far side of Flye Island. It was too far off—about a mile—for me to see Freddy, but I heard via the CB that he was safe. The boats were trying to keep the capsized vessel from sinking, and I am glad to report that they were successful. Fortunately, somebody on one of the boats had some extra clothing, so they wrung Freddy out of his wet duds and put him into something dry. At that, it must have been pretty chilling, changing clothes in sub-freezing weather in a moderate northwest breeze.

Perhaps this story illustrates why people who live in small coastal communities are a bit different from those who just commute to work every day on the Seventh Avenue subway. There is a certain homogeneity of interest and spirit here, which no longer prevails in big cities. When Freddy's boat flipped, every fisherman in sight got there as fast as his engine could push him. There was no question of "not seeing" what had happened. Also, through the magic of CB (which was not around when I was at sea), everybody in the village knew about it almost as soon as it happened, and was concerned.

Not the least of the troubles afflicting our society today is a lack of real interest and concern among people. It is true that the wonders of modern science make it possible for us to know what Mr. Reagan says half an hour after he says it, but we don't know what happened to Joe Blow who lives in a apartment on the same floor as we do—and we don't particularly care. In the cities, people watch rape, robbery, and murder on the street below their windows and nobody does anything about it—nobody gives a damn except the victim.

Small towns and villages may not have the cultural centers and all the government-provided facilities of the metropolitan areas, but they have in their people a compassion and a willingness to accept the responsibility for helping each other. This is the true reason why concerned people are drifting back to the country. They don't know the answers to the problems of the cities. I don't understand them either, and maybe running away does not help, but anyway we keep the torch alight. We take time to haul our neighbors out of the bay, and if you slide into a ditch the first person who comes along stops to help.

I'll tell you a story. Years ago when my stepson was young and thought he knew something about boats and the water, he rowed out into Naskeag harbor and found that a tide rip was taking him out beyond the island. He tugged, and sweated, and pulled, and finally got out of the current and made it ashore. All the time he was struggling, one of my less conventional townsfellows, "Shackabilly" Eaton, sat on the shore and watched him. Shack told me afterward, "I had my eye on him. If he'd got in trouble, I'd have gone after him. But I didn't see no point in embarrassing him, so I just sat a while. I weren't goin' nowhere."

Census

ONE OF THE MORE cheerful items of news to come to my attention recently was the preliminary report of the census-takers indicating that the population of Brooklin has increased by only seven people since 1970. Ten years ago it was 598, and now they guess is is 605. Even if their count is subject to an error of three percent plus or minus (as the poll-takers on TV tell us theirs are), we are still in the population bush leagues and, I hope, will stay there. There was a bit of a flap for a while because the census people, not being very knowledgeable about our local geography, included the neighboring area of South Blue Hill in our count. The Blue Hillers were indignant at being thus arbitrarily deprived of some of their long-time residents, and the tax-payers of Brooklin shocked that their taxes would be increased by the state, on the theory that more people should pay more taxes. However, these matters having been straightened out, all now is well.

A cynic avers that the reason the population of Brooklin has remained stable over the years is because every time a girl becomes pregnant, a man leaves town! Although the Town Reports do not record this interesting statistic, and are not complete for the past decade, they do show that during the past four years deaths have exceeded births by about three to one. To be precise, seventy-one deaths, against twenty-three births, so an aging population also has had something to do with it. What has happened is that newcomers ("transplants," as they are called hereabouts) have made up for the disparity between births and deaths among the old residents. I am glad the town's population is remaining stable, but I am not so happy that the figures suggest the old indigenous families are not holding their own. What the statistics indicate is that with twelve newcomers every year, the town is losing two percent of its native population annually. However, compared to most urban and suburban areas, nothing much is happening, for it would take fifty years to get a complete turnover, and by that time the children and grandchildren of the immigrants will have been born here and be natives themselves.

While politicians and labor organizers bewail the fact that Maine is becoming industrialized so slowly, most of us who live here are pretty much content with things the way they are. True, it would be helpful if there were a little more employment during the winter, but I have not seen anyone starving and I know of more than a few who look forward to winter, when they can "go on Unemployment." The lack of employment and harsh weather are what save us from being inundated by waves of settlers from more congested and crime-ridden areas to the south. I am sure some enthusiast for "progress" will say it is only people like myself who want to keep things as they are, but don't kid yourself: most, if not all, of the rural population (native or transplant) feel the same way.

There have been only four houses constructed along our road during the thirty years I have lived here on Naskeag Point, but I noticed the other day that a new hole had been punched in the bordering woodland and learned that the daughter of a neighbor planned a house there. When I asked her about it, she allowed she had such an intention in mind, but that it was going to be only a foundation for the moment. That is the way we build houses around here, one at a time, and if we don't have money for all the house, we start with the basement, and often live in it for a few years. This may sound primitive to suburbanites buying assembly-line "homes" of plywood stuck together with Elmer's glue in five-hundred-unit developments, but it has the virtue that we own all, or most, of our houses, and don't figure on selling and buying a bigger one in a couple of years to enhance our "upward mobility," as the sociologists call it. People who live in towns like Brooklin are not very mobile, upward or downward. We stay put and try to pay our taxes, and as Sammy Foss said, we "seek not for fresher founts afar, Just drop [our] bucket where [we] are."

I needed a spot of cheer, because other census statistics are far from happy. I read that after three years' gestation, thirteen federal agencies have given birth to a joint conclusion that the world is going to hell in a hand-basket, and that in the next twenty years its population will jump from 4 billion to 6.35 billion. They figured also that arable land will have increased only four percent; that oil production already has about reached its limit; that the world will lose, annually, farmland equivalent to the area of the State of Maine; that there will be a water shortage; that concentrations of carbon dioxide could warm the atmosphere enough to melt the polar ice caps; that 20 percent of all plant and animal species will be extinct; and other cheerful prophecies of like nature.

A Countryman's Farewell

148

Somehow or other I can't fit Brooklin, Maine, into this picture. I can increase my arable land one hundred percent by just turning under a bit more grass, which will save me cutting it. I doubt there will be many species made extinct around here, but if it should happen to the coons, porcupines, and blackflies, I would count it a blessing. Water is no problem. If I lose my electricity, I'll dip my water out of the well—I have one that is ten feet across. I also have a woodlot that grows faster than I can cut it, and so have most of my neighbors. Climate I can't do much about, and the prospect of the ocean in my dooryard is not really one of my overwhelming concerns at the moment; anyway, I doubt I'll be around to worry about it in twenty years. The population I have already taken care of—so, how about helping me pick some pie cherries?

Timepiece

OUR GRANDFATHER CLOCK, which has been ticking away now for a couple of hundred years, allowing for a certain amount of downtime, stopped the other day at a quarter of eleven. It gave no warning, just stopped. When I gave the pendulum a nudge, it resumed its measured swing, but only for a few minutes. I thought perhaps it needed a rest, and left it alone for a couple of days. However, when I again started it, it did no better, so I concluded something serious was wrong.

When this happened once before, about ten years ago, I called in a clock doctor who took it to the hospital and kept it for a month. When I got it back, another month was all it ran. I was discouraged. I thought that after 190 years it had seen its day, but in discussing the matter with a perfect stranger in the Hilltop Restaurant one day (I have no idea how the subject came up—all sorts of people talk to me on all sorts of subjects), I was advised to get a spray can of WD-40, give the clock's innards a good shot, and hope for the best. I did, and to my utter astonishment it worked. When I gave the pendulum a touch it resumed its old beat, and ran for ten years until a few days ago. This is not a plug for WD-40, other than to recount its ability to breathe new life into an old body, but is a suggestion that simple remedies sometimes are adequate to cure what appear to be mortal ailments.

When we took the hood off the clock this time, we gathered up enough cobwebs to spin a shroud, so perhaps they had something to do with the problem. After another shot of WD-40 the little ship above the dial, which has been steadily pitching on its two-hundred-year journey to nowhere, got under way again.

I like old things, not just because I am old (though not as old as the clock), but because most things made that long ago bear the imprint of their maker somewhere about them. I suppose two hundred years ago in Boston, where my clock was made, there were a few things turned out in quantity, but not many; certainly not clocks. I doubt any two grandfather clocks ever made were exactly alike. To begin with, a clocksmith constructed the works, and a cabinetmaker the case. Maybe they are still made that way, but not one at a time as they used to be.

When I lived in Pennsylvania I owned a grandfather clock that had been made in Bucks County. I couldn't bring it to Amen Farm because the case was eight-feet-six-inches tall and I would have had to cut a hole in the ceiling for it to fit in our low rooms. It had been made in a country town and was a good deal less sophisticated than my Boston timepiece. It ran for only thirty hours on a winding, so I placed it against the wall at the foot of the stairs, where I would be reminded to wind it every night when I went to bed. I say "wind," but actually the weights had to be hoisted up by pulling down on two chains, one for the time and the other for the chime. I forget now who made it, but he was a member of a family of clockmakers. As a matter of fact, my present clock is the product of another clock-making family. I guess the skill ran in the blood, which is why the clocks are still ticking after a couple of centuries. They were made with pride—one couldn't let the family down.

I think that sense of pride, not only in what we make but how we behave, is perhaps the greatest casualty of the days in which we live. I have on my office wall a small modern barometer. It is quite efficient, but I judge the factory that made it turns them out by the thousands, and only the men on final assembly ever see one complete. I know if this barometer stopped functioning, I would just heave it out with the trash and get a new one. It is expendable. On the wall of my living room I have another barometer, a mercurial one, made by C. Lefever in Hackney about the same time as my Boston clock. It was made lovingly and with pride of workmanship, too. It cost more when it was first made and is worth even more now. It is not that this instrument does any better job of recording the barometric pressure, but that it does it within a framework of beauty and personal achievement. Perhaps that loss is something inevitable, a sacrifice to "progress," but I am not sure we are ahead. As a matter of fact, taking all things into consideration, I am pretty sure we are dragging our anchor. That is one of the reasons I live in Maine. You can't build wooden boats or dig clams or trap lobsters or write newspaper columns on an assembly line.

Finis

A READER ONCE wrote to me asking if Amen Farm was a *real* place, or if it existed only in mind as an idea, a Utopia. He thought, perhaps, that I had better have called it Erewhon, after Samuel Butler's fantasy. Up to a point he was right, of course, because every man's life is as he imagines it to be, but the material Amen Farm is as I have described it in this and other books. Its trees sway in the wind off the bay; its flowers open in the sunshine; its lawns are green velvet decked in the morning with the gossamer webs of spiders; and long, ghostlike streamers of fog blow across its pasture. Though there are few animals these days, the spirits of those which once bore me company live on in their old haunts.

Strangely, though, when I die my dream of Amen Farm will have more permanence than its reality. Others will live here, and the place will change to accord with the times and the views of different owners. The snows and gales of winters to come will break down its fences and overthrow its lichen-covered stone walls; the trees and alders will grow and the ever-waiting little spruces will edge into its fields. There will be houses built along the roadside and new faces will be seen in the village, but my writing about it as it was will have fixed it at a point in time. A writer is like a painter, who leaves behind a picture that does not change. Gilbert White's Selborne lives on as he left it, "one single straggling street, three quarters of a mile in length, in a sheltered vale," and Parson Woodforde's study chimney continues to smoke as it did on April 27, 1789: "My study smoaked amazingly this morning . . . It always did smoke and am afraid ever will when the Wind is in the WSW." Both Parson Woodforde and his house are long gone.

Long ago I received from a friend, Andrew, whose body was old and crippled but whose spirit still burned brightly, a short letter containing a poem he had read to me over the telephone. I had not known the poem before, and I shall cherish it as a gift that I can hold in my mind long after more material presents have passed away.

Andrew lived down the coast in a small village that resembles what I imagine the Dunnet's Landing of Sarah Orne Jewett must look like. I say "must look like" rather than "must have looked like," because Dunnet's Landing had its genesis in the mind of Miss Jewett more than a hundred years ago, and so still exists, an everlasting, unchanging community that will never grow old.

Andrew and I had things in common besides our age. He recently had published a book of letters written to him by Vita Sackville-West.* They are the comfortable sort of casual communications that pass between friends. After reading them you feel somewhat more at peace with the life you live. What is unusual is that Andrew and Vita never met. Their correspondence grew out of chance and was fostered by a community of thought. What Andrew and I had in common was that we had never met either, although we talked frequently on the telephone. What kept our acquaintance going was that we also shared a community of thought. Although it would have been difficult for Andrew to go abroad to meet Vita Sackville-West, it would have been easy for me to go to "Dunnet's Landing" to see him. The reason I did not go was that in addition to the lethargy of age, something told me it is wiser not to pursue happiness to its hiding place. Lovers too often engage in this pursuit, aching with the need for total possession, which, when accomplished, looses the silver cord and breaks the golden bowl.

Today is my birthday, and I think my body must be as old as Andrew's was then, though by quite undeserved good fortune, it is in better condition. The poem he read to me is an appropriate birthday

*Collected by Dr. Nancy MacKnight, Andrew's letters from Vita were published in a book titled *Dearest Andrew* (Scribners, 1979).

reminder, as well as being a wholly charming entity. It was composed by Thomas Jones, Jr., in Peterborough, New Hampshire, early in this century.

ACROSS THE FIELDS OF YESTERDAY
HE SOMETIMES COMES TO ME!
A LITTLE BOY JUST HOME FROM SCHOOL,
A LITTLE BOY AT PLAY,
HE LOOKS AT ME SO WISTFULLY
ONCE HE HAS CREPT WITHIN—
I WONDER IF HE HOPES TO SEE
THE MAN I MIGHT HAVE BEEN!

I suppose each of us coming to the sunset years wonders about the person he might have been. Much of everyone's life is ordained by circumstance, but there is no one who does not have some margin for the operation of free will.

Somewhere in his journals, Thoreau says that his neighbors (Minott and his sister) owned about ten acres of woodlot they had been cutting off for thirty years, and that Minott allowed they could continue to do so for as long as they should live. Thoreau wrote that his neighbor knew every tree on the land, from saplings to mature timber, and could guide it as he chose. I guess it is that way with our lives. We cannot magically change poplars into oak trees, but we can be selective in our choices so that in our old age that little boy will not be too disappointed even if he knows he could have done better.

Such fragile immortality as we have is stored in books and in the minds of those who knew us. I suppose in the future it also will be stored in cans of film and on tape and computer disks, but I think books will ever be the individual man's key to his past. I can still feel my own childhood, and see the ancient house and garden of my grandparents. I can picture my grandmother's fat cob standing with her head over the stable half-door. I can conjure up the smells of the kitchen and the odor of my grandfather's brandy and cigars; but, except where I have recorded them, they are gone into the darkness. My own grandchildren have similar memories of Amen Farm, and with what I have written, their grandchildren, not yet born, will share experiences of what had been before their time.

In a recent volume of letters of Logan Pearsall Smith, collected by Edwin Tribble, Smith notes that he has been reading *Don Quixote*, and that he has found there "the epitaph which I should like to be mine at my decease: 'Though he achieved not great things, yet did he die in their pursuit.'"

I found this to be a fascinating book; I should like to suggest that the pursuit of small things, which make up most of our lives, can be as rewarding as the seeking of great ones. I say this because as I look back over my own life, I find it is an accumulation of events that are unimportant individually, but cheerful indeed to look back upon collectively and to record. The memories I spoke of in the first part of this essay are, none of them, great events—but as Matthew Arnold said,

IS IT SO SMALL A THING,

TO HAVE ENJOYED THE SUN,

TO HAVE LIVED LIGHT IN THE SPRING,

TO HAVE LOVED, TO HAVE THOUGHT, TO HAVE DONE;

TO HAVE ADVANCED TRUE FRIENDS, AND BEAT DOWN BAFFLING FOES.

I offer the following as an old man's birthday gift. It was written by Thomas Bird Mosher, whose name will be remembered as long as fine books are treasured. It is titled "When Finis Comes," and is to be found in *Amphora II*, published in Portland, Maine, in 1926.

SWEETHEART, 'TIS TRUE STARS RISE AND SET,

AND ALL FAIR SEASONS CEASE TO BE.

THE SUNLIGHT FADES FROM OFF THE SEA,

AND WINTERY WINDS OUR ROSE LEAVES FRET.

YET PAST THE REACH OF BARREN HOURS

ACROSS THE YEARS ARE SHINING YET

YOUR FACE AND EYES—CAN I FORGET

THEIR LOVELY LIGHT THAT SHONE ON ME?

NAY, SWEET, THESE CHANGE NOT, THESE ABIDE

BEYOND THE STRESS OF TIME AND TIDE,

ACROSS THE YEARS IN YOUTH'S FAIR CLIME
LIVE ALL LOST LOVES AND ALL DEAD FLOWERS,—
THE LAND OF MEMORY KNOWS NO TIME.

When I was young, conversations were much more allusive than they are today, and it was commonplace for educated people to recite snippets of poetry, or even long passages, to illustrate some point of conversation. Nowadays, if you recite a couple of lines of poetry your listeners fidget and are embarrassed. Of course, people seldom quote poetry now, for most studies are purged of any association with English, as though knowledge of it suggests that students have been wasting their time on nonproductive matters. The few lovers of poetry there are can be found among the old, of course, and also the quite young. Librarians of all ages I rank high on the list. For them especially, and for all my old friends I offer, because I love its bittersweet reminder, Austin Dobson's "Paradox of Time."

TIME GOES, YOU SAY? AH NO!
ALAS, TIME STAYS, WE GO

or, as the French poet de Ronsard said it,

LE TEMPS S'EN VA, LE TEMPS S'EN VA, MA DAME!
LAS! LE TEMPS NON: MAIS NOUS NOUS EN ALLONS!

l'Envoi

And will any say when my bell of quittance
is heard in the gloom,
And a crossing breeze cuts a pause in its
outrollings,
Till they rise again, as they were a new bell's boom,
"He hears it not now, but used to notice such things"?
                    —*From "Afterwards" by Thomas Hardy*

A Countryman's Farewell
156